D0412435

MISS SAVIDGE MOVES HER HOUSE

Christine Adams now runs a bed and breakfast in Ware House in Norfolk.

Michael McMahon is a writer and prison chaplain, whose recent books include *My Friend the Enemy* (with Paul Briscoe; also published by Aurum) and *Saints: the Art, the History, the Inspiration*.

'The remarkable true story of a gutsy spinster'
Eastern Daily Press

'An amazing project . . . a truly remarkable woman'
SPY

'The desire to honour a dying Aunt's wishes became something deeply personal'
Woman's Weekly

'Write funny story of furniture in attic (a life)'

Note written to herself by May Savidge, on a scrap of paper found in a box in the attic of Ware Hall-House

MISS SAVIDGE MOVES HER HOUSE

Christine Adams

with Michael McMahon

A note from the authors

All quotations in this book are given with their original punctuation. Miss Savidge wrote letters in carefully constructed prose, but her diaries were written as notes.

The names of two or three people have been changed in order to avoid causing embarrassment or offence. Miss Savidge would not have wanted a book written in her honour to hurt anyone.

First published in Great Britain
under the title A Lifetime in the Building
2009 by Aurum Press Ltd
74 77 White Lion Street,
London
www.aurumpress.co.uk

Copyright © Christine Adams and Michael McMahon 2009

This paperback edition first published in 2010 by Aurum Press

Christine Adams and Michael McMahon have asserted their moral right to be identified as the
Authors of this Work in accordance with the Copyright Designs and Patents Act 1988.

All rights reserved. No part of this book may be reproduced or utilised in any form or by any means,
electronic or mechanical, including photocopying, recording or by any information storage and
retrieval system, without permission in writing from Aurum Press Ltd.

Every effort has been made to trace the copyright holders of material quoted in this book.
If application is made in writing to the publisher, any omissions will be included in future editions.

A catalogue record for this book is available from the British Library.

ISBN 978 1 84513 518 8

Typeset by SX Composing DTP, Rayleigh, Essex
Printed and bound by CPI Group (UK) Ltd, Croydon, CR0 4YY

I dedicate this book to my amazing children, Daniel and Polly, who have helped me through eight tough years. With their help, and the support of my wonderful friends, I have fulfilled my promise.

Christine Adams

THE SUNDAY NEWS, DECEMBER 3, 1978

n joggers
being 'ı

RHODESIAN joggers seems to
craze sweeping America an
is too scarce to import su

THE HOUSE THAT MISS MAY REBUILT

MISS May Savidge (67),
has almost single-handedly
moved her two-storey cot-
tage brick by brick from its
location 160 km away and
rebuilt it at Wells-next-the-
Sea, Norfolk.

She learnt 11 years ago
that local officials planned
to pull down her 500-year-
old cottage, which then
stood near the village of
Monkey Row, to make way
for a roundabout.

"The house was too
valuable to destroy," said
Miss Savidge, a retired
book illustrator. "I simply
decided to take it with me
and rebuild it."

She has spent every day
from dawn to dusk for the
past 11 years moving the
house. She numbered and
relaid all 10 000 bricks and
8 000 roof tiles herself.
She paid to have the materials moved by lorry.

The house is now almost
finished and Miss Savidge,
who is living in a caravan
on the site, expects to move
in by Christmas with her
cat Pansey and dog Sasha.
Iana-Reuter.

"BRICK BY BRICK" again

Originally dated
oak frame &
lath & plaster (NO BRICKS)

Dear Miss ~~Savage~~ Savidges
    Please find enclosed one
antique nail. My husband got it
when he was in the building
trade, now retired in ill health.
I admire your grits immensley,
it spurs me on to get jobs done
myself around my modern bungalow.
I hope I shall be able to view
your house from the outside when
I can get to Norfolk. I hope to
go to Walsingham, Raynham Manor
Norwich & Naunton Hall.
        Yours Faithfully
                ...do (MKS age 57½)

REMEMBER to use the POST CODE!

Miss May Savidge.
(who re-moved and re-built her house)
WELLS-NEXT-THE-SEA.

Norfolk

Contents

It has been impossible to mention all the people who helped May in her daunting task. A few have been named, but if you read this book and know that you were there, in her many hours of need, I sincerely thank you and hope you enjoy reminiscing about your part in the life of an extraordinary woman.

INTRODUCTION

by Paul Atterbury,
BBC Antiques Roadshow

The Antiques Roadshow is one of Britain's best-loved and most familiar television programmes, yet this perennially popular series still has a few secrets. One of these is something called the Furniture Round, when one of the experts visits the homes of members of the public who have contacted the BBC about large things they are unable to bring to the show. Every Roadshow has a Furniture Round, which is usually spread over a radius of fifty miles around the location and takes place in the days that immediately precede the recording day. A few of the Roadshow team of experts do these Rounds, and they are well versed in the techniques of talking to the owners of the objects under review without giving anything away.

A few years ago I was given the task of carrying out the Furniture Round for the show that was to be filmed at Holkham Hall, in Norfolk. Over the allocated three days a colleague and I visited everyone who had written in for that particular Round, and we were well on the way to completing the final selection of the few things that we would be able to bring in to help the owners. As ever, there were a couple of unresolved issues, usually visits that could not be made because the owners had gone away. One of these was in Wells-next-the-Sea, to a lady who had written in about a desk with some association with Mark Twain. From the photograph it did not look very exciting, but we had persevered, telephoning regularly throughout the three days, partly because the address, Ware Hall-House, sounded promising. There was never an answer and no means of leaving a message.

On the evening of the final day, as we were tying up the loose ends, we decided to give it a final go, and called the number again. Rather to our surprise, there was an answer, and we arranged to visit the lady, who had been away for a few days and had forgotten about her letter to the BBC, immediately. We parked on the green at the heart of Wells and walked up the narrow path that we had been told to follow. There was no sign of any house, just an old door in a high wall. We entered, and were faced at once by what was obviously a major timber-framed building of the medieval era. Yet, somehow it did not look quite right and I was intrigued.

The lady who opened the door introduced herself as Christine Adams and led us in, to show us the desk that was the reason for the visit. As I had guessed, it was relatively unexciting. At that point, I decided I had to put my BBC duties aside, and told Christine I had to know about the house. She asked us if we had plenty of time, which we had, offered us some tea and took us into the wooden conservatory that projected from one side. As soon as we were seated, she launched into the long and complicated story of May Savidge.

She told us about May and her extraordinary life, about the house which she had demolished and rebuilt, and about her compulsive collecting and hoarding. Christine also explained where she fitted in, and how she had devoted much of her life to fulfilling the wishes of an eccentric and demanding woman who was her former husband's aunt. I was completely gripped, not least by Christine's lengthy entanglement in a project that was actually nothing to do with her.

When we left, some hours later, having toured the house and looked at what remained of Auntie May's collections, I knew that we had a story that had to be included in the Roadshow. The challenge was how to do it. It broke all the rules. There was no object to talk about, other than the house and that could not be taken to the show. It was a multi-layered story of great complexity that seemed to demand much more time than the normal few minutes taken up by a typical Roadshow item. And at the heart of it was Christine who was understandably reluctant to expose the extraordinary story of her life to the Roadshow's cameras. She was happy to talk about Auntie May and the house, but it took me a while to persuade her that her story was just as exciting. In the event, we made it work somehow, without breaking the Roadshow's rules about items having to be unprepared and unrehearsed, and when it was transmitted some months later, it provoked a great response, with many people wanting to know more about May Savidge, her house and the story.

Through this process, I came to know Christine quite well, helped by the filming of a follow-up item for the end-of-series Roadshow retrospective programme, which involved more visits to the house and gave me the opportunity to stay there and experience Auntie May's handiwork in a more direct way.

From the very start of this adventure, I knew that what the story really demanded was a book. Television, as ever, could only scratch the surface. I did my best to encourage Christine to write it all down, and to collect together photographs and other material that could bring it all to life. Above all else, I encouraged her to tell her story, which seemed to me in so many ways the most interesting part of the whole saga. During our conversations, I had become aware that Christine was in some ways a prisoner, trapped both by the story and the house. There were many ghosts to be laid, and I was sure that the process of writing it all down would in some ways release her.

This book, which I read in one sitting, seems to me to have done just that. It is exciting, enthralling and occasionally shocking. And through it Christine Adams seems to have gained her freedom. She is the real heroine of the story and a remarkable woman who can now see beyond the limits on her life imposed by Ware Hall-House, which, in the final analysis, is nothing to do with her.

It has often been said that *The Antiques Roadshow* is not just a popular television programme, but something with the power to affect people and the way they live. Christine Adams, and the story of Auntie May, has changed my life, and I like to think that we have changed hers. I am so glad we persevered and kept trying that telephone number.

Paul Atterbury, April 2009

CHAPTER ONE

An End and a Beginning

April 1993

She looked so frail and broken in her tidily arranged bed. I picked up her hand and held it. It was blue. There was no weight in it. The nurse said: 'I don't think she can feel her hands any more. Why don't you stroke her neck? And do talk to her: she's slipping away fast now, but hearing is the last sense to go . . .'

It seemed cruel that someone so fiercely independent should have to die like this. Auntie May should have been the one doing the nursing, not the one being nursed. She was a giver, not a taker. When she had joined the St John Ambulance Brigade in 1938, she had taken both its mottoes – 'For the Faith', and 'For The Service of Mankind' – as her own. She had tended the sick and the wounded, visited the handicapped and housebound, given and organised first aid courses, and run fundraising and recruiting events. Years later, when the Wells Cottage Hospital had been listed for closure, she joined in the battle to keep it open for the benefit of the community; now, aged not quite eighty-two, she was dying in the very Norfolk hospital she had fought to save for others. It just didn't seem right.

•

I first met Auntie May in 1966, when she was fifty-four.* Strictly speaking, she wasn't my aunt, she was my husband's, but he introduced me to her as Auntie May, and I've thought of her as my own auntie ever since. Tony clearly regarded her with affection, but he did warn me that the family thought her eccentric. His mother, Nellie, May's sister, was very fond of her, too, but whenever May's name was mentioned, her eyes would widen – though she wouldn't quite raise them to heaven – and she would say: 'May! Whatever will she get up to next?' She wasn't a typical maiden aunt.

Nellie told me that when she was still in her mid-teens, May met an older man, a Shakespearean actor; later, they planned to marry, but he died in 1938. Nellie said she never recovered from the loss, and that the signet ring she wore on her wedding finger had been his. Shortly after his death, she had joined the St John Ambulance Brigade and thrown all her energy into it. During the war, she had retrained as a technical draughtswoman and had helped to design the Mosquito. She had been the only female in the team.

Then, when the war was over and the nation faced a housing shortage, May thought it wouldn't be fair for a single woman to occupy a house all to herself, so she bought an old Thames river bus, the *Formosa*, and converted it into a floating home. She did some of the conversion work herself, but she never managed to make the boat's hull totally watertight, and in 1947 she abandoned it for another restoration project, a house that would otherwise have fallen down. It was a semi-derelict, semi-detached cottage – 1 Monkey Row, Ware, Hertfordshire, that had originally been built as a 'hall house': a medieval arrangement in which private living

* May Alice Savidge was born in Streatham on 25 May 1911.

space is attached to an open hall.* The council had told her that her house was to be demolished to make way for a relief road and May had dug her heels in and resolved to save the building at all costs. It would be a fight that would occupy the rest of her life.

But when I met Auntie May for that first time, I was surprised: she looked nothing like the person that Tony and his mother had led me to expect. In my mind's eye, I had imagined a bag lady in wellington boots, but Auntie May came to our wedding in a neat tapestry suit with a matching pillbox hat. In our wedding photographs, she looks elegant, happy and relaxed.

This very positive first impression was confirmed by her choice of wedding present – though it was the first of many signs that showed she had an unconventional approach to life. She gave us a home-made first aid kit, containing items that she had chosen herself. It was a particularly appropriate gift, for Tony and I had planned to drive to the Sahara and back for our honeymoon. Tony – who has more than a small share of the Savidge family's independence of spirit – had bought a long-wheel-base truck and converted it into a motorhome, and we took it across Europe to the Middle East, returning via north Africa. Auntie May's first aid kit contained something for every imaginable emergency. There were splints, slings and bandages for injuries, medicines for food poisoning – and there was even a tourniquet for snakebites.

I took to Auntie May immediately. She was certainly a character. There was something strong, and centred and certain about her – but something kind and gentle, too. I remember being surprised to find her shy. It seemed strange that someone who had ploughed such an independent furrow should be so undemon-

---

* When she re-erected the building, she named it Ware Hall-House, not Ware Hall House; the hyphen emphasises that it is an example of this particular architectural style.

strative and softly spoken. I was happy to have her as an auntie. I felt proud of her and yet, at the same time, there was something about her that made me feel protective – though I could see that it wouldn't be a good idea to show it.

Our honeymoon was a great adventure – though that's another story – and the next time I met Auntie May was the following spring, when Tony took me down to see her in the cottage she was fighting to save from demolition. It was obvious that her time in Ware was running out. The building that was 1 Monkey Row and 36 Baldock Street now stood in a rubble-strewn car park. Auntie May's half looked presentable enough, but the other side, which had been a bakery, looked long abandoned.* I remember peering through its grubby shop-front window. The place was empty, apart from a dusty glass cabinet containing a couple of brown and white bowls and jugs.

But when we stepped inside Auntie May's half, we found a very different ambience. It was warm and cosy, and full of an incredible quantity of clutter. Every surface was piled high with so many bits and pieces that it looked like an overstocked curiosity shop. There were books, ornaments and mementos everywhere. Tony told me that there was much, much more stuff like it – everything from a stripped-down motorbike to a vast collection of matchboxes – in the two-storey workshop at the bottom of the garden. Tony and I had brought our honeymoon slides to show her and when we asked where we could plug in our projector, she pointed to the light socket hanging from the centre of the room. It was a monkey-puzzle of interconnected two-way adapters, from which wires ran in every direction. Tony said that if we plugged anything else into it, the circuit would blow. But Auntie May insisted – and there was

---

* I later learned that it had been empty since the local council purchased it in 1959.

4

indeed a bang, a flash and a puff of smoke. She seemed to have a blind spot when it came to electricity.

Auntie May didn't show us the workshop, but she did show us around the house. She was proud of it. She had stripped out the 'improvements' of several centuries to expose features that showed the building to be ancient. She had uncovered a window that had been identified as fifteenth century. She had exposed heavy oak beams that bore the marks of medieval carpenters. She had lifted crumbling lino to reveal the wide, oak floorboards that those carpenters had cut by hand. She had uncovered fireplaces that were unmistakably Tudor. And when she had shown what she had found to architectural historians, they had told her she was living in a building that was a fine example of a medieval hall house. It was a rare example, too, for most hall-houses are considerably larger.

Auntie May told us she was determined to save such an important part of national heritage even if she had to take it apart beam by beam and board by board, and rebuild it in another part of the country. She had been looking at possible sites in Devon or Cornwall, but was now thinking of moving to Norfolk. She had spent several happy holidays there in the past, and she had found a plot of land, an old rope-walk garden in Wells-next-the-Sea, on the North Norfolk coast, where ships' rigging had been made for generations. The idea seemed half-crazy, but I did think that if anyone could do it, Auntie May could. After all, she had done a pretty good job renovating the house where it stood.

And so, in 1969, when the bulldozers finally reached her front gate, Auntie May had taken the building to pieces and moved it a hundred miles to Norfolk – and set about rebuilding it with her own hands. 'That house!' Nellie would exclaim; it was a project she dismissed as bordering on madness.

Now, twenty-three years later, Auntie May was dying, and 'that house' was still far from finished. The walls were up and the roof was on, but the place was little more than a shaky shell. There were no internal partitions upstairs, and many of the windows were just timber frames covered in plastic sheets. And the building was filled from top to bottom with boxes containing a lifetime's accumulated junk. So was the outhouse and the caravan in which May had lived for years, and the garden contained almost as much again, piled up under makeshift polythene shelters that were half-buried in nettles and brambles. God only knew what all those boxes might contain. Sorting them all out would be somebody's nightmare, to say nothing of the work still to be done to the building itself. Tony and I had only just finished rebuilding our own home, a cottage in Cambridgeshire that we had worked hard on for years, and in recent years, as we had watched May's project slow down and seem more and more hopeless, he had said to me many times: 'Don't ever let me take on that house!'

I leaned over her, stroking her neck. Then Auntie May opened her eyes and struggled to speak. She had just enough strength left for her face to show anxiety. 'Sorry,' she said.

I didn't know what she meant. What had she got to apologise for? She had done nothing in her lifetime that had caused me pain or hurt. I opened my mouth to say something comforting and non-committal, but the words that came were not the words I planned to speak. It was one of those moments when you seem to have stepped outside yourself, and have no control over what you hear yourself saying.

'Don't worry, Auntie May, whatever you want us to do, we'll do; whatever your final wishes are, we'll carry them out. I promise.' She sighed and closed her eyes. She seemed at peace.

Then it struck me why May might have felt the need to say sorry. Surely she hadn't left us the house?

CHAPTER TWO

An Extraordinary Inheritance

In which I describe what we found in Ware Hall-House
after Auntie May's death

I bought lilies for the funeral. We stopped off at Ware Hall-House
before the service. The place was damp, and dark, and lifeless.
Wind had torn away the plastic that May had used to cover the
window frames that hadn't yet been glazed, and when we pushed
open the front door, we could tell the weather had started to get in,
for there was a musty, earthy smell – like mushrooms in a damp
paper bag. There was something else in the atmosphere, too: a
feeling of absence. The place felt abandoned. It didn't seem right
to leave it unattended. I went back to the car, got the flowers, found
a vase and put them on Auntie May's table, beside her clock. Their
strong, sweet scent lingered for weeks.

The will was read to Tony and me, and to Auntie May's
executors, Betty Leftley and Pat Terrington, in the Wells office of
the solicitors Hayes & Storr. The firm occupies a Georgian-fronted
building just across the village green, known as 'the Buttlands',
and is very near Ware Hall-House. The street it stands on is called
Chancery Lane. I hadn't noticed the name before: it made me smile.
The contrast between the great thoroughfare at the heart of
London's legal district and a narrow alleyway in a north Norfolk

seaside town couldn't be greater. For some reason, the name made me think of Charles Dickens, and shortly after we climbed the dark, narrow stairs to the first-floor office, and the solicitor had placed two large, decrepit and very dusty leather handbags on to the table, I found myself wondering whether I hadn't walked into a scene from one of his novels.

The will wasn't quite as complicated as the one in *Bleak House*, but there was definitely something Dickensian about it. It ran to eight pages and listed scores of family heirlooms, each with a carefully recorded provenance. I still have a copy of it:

4. I GIVE the following items free of inheritance tax:

(1) To my sister Nellie Henrietta Adams . . . (knowing that she would not want my house*) or if she shall predecease me then to the said Anthony Brian Adams, the following jewellery which came to me from our mother Henrietta Geertruida Carolina Augusta Savidge (born Hovelson) or from our grandmother Cornelia Johanna Hovelson (born Kikkert) or from our great-grandmother Maria Adriana Judith Kikkert (born Coninck Westenberg) namely:

(a) My gold chain – approximately fifty-five inches long with watch clip . . .

(n) My striking clock black enamel on iron with a lion's head at each end and a gilt cream face, made in USA – approximately fifteen inches times ten inches high which was a wedding present to our father and mother (twenty-eighth July one thousand nine hundred and six) from his father and mother (Joseph Traylor Savidge and Sarah Savidge, born Hampson) together with winding key which is in my large brown purse . . .

---

* This is something of an understatement!

5. I GIVE to the said Anthony Brian Adams free of inheritance tax:

(2) The following items all of which are from my mother's family:

(a) The christening shawl used in the Kikkert family [her Dutch ancestors on her mother's side] since one thousand eight hundred and fifteen or thereabouts . . .

(k) My old wooden black box – sixteen and a half inches times ten inches times eleven inches high, with handle on top, which probably belonged to my grandmother Cornelia Johanna Hovelsen (born Kikkert), which has a left-hand lock and a key which is in my large brown purse and contains the following paintings by my grandfather Joseph Traylor Savidge:

(i) Full-length portrait of King Edward VIII – five and three-quarter inches times three and a half inches . . .

The will goes on for page after page like this, but at the time, it all went by in a blur, because Tony and I were sitting there pole-axed by section 3 (1), which confirmed my guess and his worst fear:

I GIVE free of inheritance tax my freehold house situated and known as Ware Hall-House, Water Pit Lane, Wells-next-the-Sea, aforesaid . . . to my trustees upon trust for my nephew Anthony Brian Adams of The Nook, South Street, Litlington, near Royston, in the county of Hertford, during his life and after his death upon trust for such of his children living at the death of my said nephew . . .

(2) I DIRECT that my nephew shall during his lifetime at his own expense keep the house . . . in good repair and condition . . .

Even though it wasn't a complete surprise, it was still a shock. Auntie May had not only left us the house, she had left us the task of finishing it off. We couldn't sell it; we were stuck with it. And we couldn't leave it as it was — it wasn't even watertight. As the list of other bequests rolled on, Betty and Pat must have picked up the uncomfortable atmosphere. One of them — I can't now remember which — said: 'This is family business — we shouldn't really be here.'

The atmosphere continued during the car journey back to Litlington and we spent the next couple of days in a worried trance. Then, one day, we decided we had to bite the bullet. We packed the car with sleeping bags, hot-water bottles, extra jumpers and a primus stove, and set off for Wells.

We had a pretty good idea of what lay ahead of us: we had been to Ware Hall-House only a fortnight ago. Even so, when we opened the gate in the garden wall, we were shocked. Briars now reached beyond the first-floor windows. The house seemed somehow tattier. The garden seemed far more densely packed with clutter. I don't suppose that the amount had actually increased since we had last seen it. When we had been there before, we had given our attention to the person living in the middle of it all; now, there was nothing to look at but her junk.

There was so much of it in the house that we could hardly get in. The front door wouldn't open fully, because right behind it was a pale green 1930s kitchen unit. Tony opened its doors, to find that it contained hundreds of neatly stacked empty jam jars, large and small, ancient and modern, glass and pottery. Behind it, the passage was blocked by a great heap of chairs — a tangle of rusty springs, fraying upholstery and broken arms and legs. We squeezed past them into the great hall, which was filled with boxes and trunks stacked up to the ceiling, with narrow alleys left between them. Tony followed one that led to a window and pulled off the battens that held up the sheet of stained polythene covering its unglazed frame. Spring sunshine tumbled in – just as it does when Pip tears down Miss Havisham's curtains in the 1940s film of *Great Expectations*. It fell like a floodlight on the far corner of the room, in which half a dozen or so headless figures were suspended – coats hanging on hooks fixed in the ceiling. I fiddled my way through the cartons and rusty tin trunks to get a closer look, and saw that one of the hangers carried a St John Ambulance uniform jacket. When I took its cuff in my hand, the sleeve fell in pieces to the floor.

I don't know how long we were transfixed by the atmosphere of the place, but at some point, Tony reminded me that we had come to sort things out, not to gawp – and so we set to work. We started on the chairs. As we disentangled them, we found that nearly all of them were broken. They were all, however, interesting pieces of furniture – at least, they once had been. We struggled with them for the whole morning, shifting them into heaps of matching or near-matching sets, and stacks of chairs worth repairing and beyond repair. When, after a couple of hours, we stood back and looked at what we had achieved, we laughed as it dawned on us that we had achieved precisely nothing. We had just replaced one pile of junk with another. Tony said that he wondered whether sorting through all this rubbish was a waste of time, and we might do better to set light to it all where it was. I am not now entirely sure he was joking. But the only thing we did set light to that evening was the Rayburn, and that took a lot of effort to get going. Once Tony had coaxed it into life, we walked around the corner to the Crown, where we washed in hot water and enjoyed a hearty meal. It was a routine that we were to follow for some years to come – though we didn't realise then quite how many of those years there would be.

A hard day's work, a good supper and a few drinks should have set us up for a well-earned sleep, but our first night in Ware

Hall-House didn't go quite as comfortably as we had planned. We set out our sleeping bags in the space that would eventually be the main bedroom, but one of the walls was still open studwork and the door hadn't yet been hung. This wouldn't have mattered if it hadn't been for the rats. We knew they were about, because we had the rat man come before our arrival and he had found evidence of them everywhere. We didn't fancy being visited by rats as we slept, so Tony built us in and them out by nailing sheets of perspex to the inside of the studwork. When he had fixed the last piece over the doorway, we felt safe. But not for long.

We had only just climbed into our sleeping bags when we heard scuffling and scratching noises from the ground floor. 'Rats!' said Tony, cheerfully, but then the scuffling and scratching got louder. There must have been scores of them. We could hear them fighting over the little plastic trays in which the rat man had put out his poisoned bait. The sound of plastic scraping on concrete echoed around the house. I looked at Tony and his face wasn't quite so cheerful. I expect mine was showing terror. I certainly felt it. Without speaking, Tony reached across to the pile of tools we had been using, picked up a claw hammer and passed me a hand axe. We sat up for what seemed like ages, until the scrabbling noises faded away and we could no longer fight off sleep.

When I woke up the next morning, my first thought was that I had been having a nightmare, until I turned over and found myself lying on an axe. I sat up and looked around me. What on earth were we doing here, sleeping in a building site? We had endured only one night of it, but Auntie May had been roughing it like this – and much worse – for twenty-three years. I got up, stretched and pulled away the sheet of perspex that had served as a door. The rest of the first floor had no boards down and I could see all Auntie

May's junk heaped up as high as the joists. How could she – how could anyone – live like this?

Then the birds began to sing in the overgrown garden, and I heard sparrows hopping and skipping on the tiles above my head. As I stood there, watching the morning sun spilling in to fill the gaps between the boxes that May had crammed with all the things she had been sure she would one day find a use for, the answer came to me. May had had hope. I felt her hope rise within me. We would complete her task. I was sure of it.

CHAPTER THREE

A Matter of Record

In which I discover Auntie May's diaries and
realise their significance

In the spring and summer of 1994, we came back to Ware Hall-
House every weekend. Mind, we never again heard any rats – the
poison must have worked. They had certainly tucked into it keenly
enough! We did, however, hear other creatures in the house –
creatures that Auntie May had unknowingly brought with her from
Ware. One night at the end of April, we found ourselves lying
awake listening to a noise that sounded like distant pneumatic
drills, but which seemed to be coming from somewhere indoors.
When we got up the next morning to investigate, we spotted a
couple of brown insects walking along a dusty oak beam. We had
death watch beetles. When we found out how much it would cost
to eradicate them, we decided we could live with them.*

By then, the project had taken hold of us and as the months went
by, it tightened its grip. On Friday nights, as soon as Tony came
home from work, we would pack up and head off in our Land
Rover to Wells, let some air into the house, light the Rayburn and
pop around the corner to have supper in the Crown. On Saturday

---

* I still do!

mornings, we would drive to Jewson's to pick up whatever building materials we needed for that weekend's tasks. The first was to sort out the plumbing. The downstairs loo worked well enough and there was a cold-water tap over the sink in the scullery – though we had to empty the room of boxes and boxes of junk to get comfortable access to it. It was the upstairs bathroom that was the problem – not that there was actually a room around the loo and the old, cast-iron bath above which a huge, ancient electric water heater was tied with binder twine to a beam. We ripped the whole lot out and threw it in a skip.

It was on one of those early visits that I heard my first nightingale. It was a still, late spring night and I was lying in May's bed with the windows open when I heard the most wonderful sounds coming from the little clearing we had made in the front garden. The song was sweet and pure and various: trilling, chirping, chattering and whistling. The gaps between the phrases were filled with a kind of awestruck silence, as if the rest of nature was holding its breath until the performance finished. On another occasion, I was cutting my way past the old apple tree that stood – that still stands – near the western corner of the house, when a blackbird flew up and settled on a branch a couple of feet from my face. It stood there, looking at me, and I stood there, looking back. We can only have been staring at each other for a second or two, but it was one of those moments when time seems to stop. A strange thought alighted and lingered. Was this May, making a fleeting, reassuring visit, telling me that she was at last at peace?

A couple of wing beats and it was gone – and a second, less fanciful thought occurred to me. So that was why May had always refused to let us cut down the weeds for her. She had wanted them left for the birds. She hadn't kept a garden; she had kept a wildlife sanctuary. In the summer, it was full of birdsong, butterflies and bees . The atmosphere was magical.

But we had to break the spell in order to work on the house. The nettles on either side of the path now touched each other, and the shed and Auntie May's old caravan were invisible through the tall, tumbling tangle of undergrowth that filled the site from wall to wall and fence to fence. We knew that somewhere under it all there were piles of building materials that we would want to use, including all the panes of glass Auntie May had carefully removed and labelled in 1969. We would need them to make the house properly weathertight before the next winter.

So, we set to, hacking and slashing towards where we knew the caravan to be. But the task was even harder than it looked. On only my second or third swipe, my hook struck something heavy and metallic – a stack of scaffolding poles, as it turned out – and once I had worked my way round those, I hit something solid again: an ancient mangle. The ground was almost entirely covered in junk. The brambles, briars and nettles had grown through it all, knitting it to the soil. The only way to get through was by cutting down what I could with the hook, then using a hand fork and a trowel to scrape away at the ground like an archaeologist. Working like this, I unearthed four fireplaces and grates, and two huge bread-oven doors, all of them beautifully made and finely decorated – but useless. Auntie May had rebuilt her house without a chimney. There was no need for fireplaces. They were just things that had come into her possession and were thus destined to be kept.

The caravan was only twenty yards from the house, but it took us all morning to reach it. Apart from the scaffold poles, none of the stuff that we uncovered could be of any use. We did find a neat stack of ancient floorboards, but when we tried to pick them up they turned to dust. When we finally reached the caravan, her name was still visible in the paintwork that was peeling off in patches: Blue Lady. We cut our way carefully to the door, turned the handle and pulled. It was unlocked.

The last time we had peeped inside – some twenty years earlier – the stove had been lit, the kettle was boiling on top of it and one of May's cats had been curled up sunning itself in the window. Today, the place stank of damp. The fibreboard walls and ceilings were soft and sagging. We couldn't get in for all the stuff that May had stored there. It was stacked front to back and side to side with boxes, chests and cupboards. Under the table were several piles of old 78-rpm gramophone records. When Tony reached in to pull a couple out, the paper covers came to pieces in his hands. The edges of the discs were covered in tiny silver snail trails, but the snails themselves were nowhere to be seen. We soon worked out why. As we pulled out all the clutter, we found rat-holes in the floorboards. And when we looked under the caravan, we saw several neat wheels of carefully woven grass – rats' nests. Each was filled to the brim with the unbroken, empty shells of snails.

We pulled out all the caravan's contents, and stood there looking at it, set out on the stumps and stubble of the clearing that we had made. None of the furniture was worth keeping, but we thought we ought to go through cupboards before we burned them. I am very glad we did. One old wooden cabinet contained several cardboard boxes labelled 'SJAB'. In them, we found all of Auntie May's St John Ambulance papers, dating back to the certificate qualifying her to render 'first aid to the injured' in September 1938. There was a pile of cashbooks recording every financial transaction of the Ware branch of the SJAB. There were rolled up wartime recruiting posters depicting angelically beautiful SJAB nurses, at work against the background of the London Blitz. There were all of May's personal record cards, noting her annual refresher courses in first aid, the number of divisional instruction meetings attended (forty-four of them in 1941; fifty-one in 1965), the number of hours she contributed to public and other duties, and the dates on which she was awarded her service chevrons (1942, 1945, 1948 and 1951). There were her medals and her belt buckles wrapped in tissue paper. There was the certificate recording her appointment as a divisional superintendent in Ware, dated 9 June 1958. There were photos of first aid demonstrations, newspaper cuttings and minute books. There were folders of correspondence relating to Auntie May's wartime service medal and bars. One box contained a dozen or so unworn nurses' bonnets, a pile of unissued black uniform stockings and several starched, white detachable cuffs. Another contained three blue uniform dresses and her uniform hat with cockade.

Everywhere we looked, we found hoards of things stored according to various themes. In the crumbling brick and tile shed at the northern end of the garden, we found ancient boat lights, railway lamps, Tilley lamps and hurricane lanterns, ornate Victorian paraffin lamps – one with a beautifully engraved bat etched on the chimney. Beside them were all kinds of tools, ancient and not-quite modern: hammers, axes, saws, chisels, files, clamps, cramps, spokeshaves and any number of implements that we couldn't identify. There were lengths of chain, coils of rope and all sorts of bits and pieces of brass that looked as if they had once been attached to a boat. And behind them all we found the rusty frame of the old Velocette motorcycle that Auntie May had bought during the war.

In a corner of the garden, under a cover of old gabardine mackintoshes and yellowing polythene, we found a stack of side-saddles. I pulled out one, then another, then another, then another . . . there were nine of them in varying stages of decay. How on earth would Auntie May have come by nine side-saddles? She had, as far as I knew, never ridden a horse – though I had seen the back end of what looked like a stuffed one among the heap of furniture in the front passage of the house. I wondered if there might be any connection, so I spent some time shifting chairs and wardrobes so I could get a better look. When I got to it, though, it turned out to be some kind of vaulting horse – at least, that's what I thought at first. When I looked more closely, I realised it couldn't be. There was a carpeted step on one side to allow someone to mount it, and the top wasn't straight, like a piece of gym equipment, but indented, like the back of a real horse. I dragged in one of the saddles. It fitted perfectly. But what was it for? And why were there eight more? I couldn't work it out.

Some long time later, we had a visitor who knew a bit about horses and so we asked her what all that horsey stuff meant. 'Do you have any painters in the family?' she asked. Tony said yes: his great-grandfather had been a portrait painter, but that we didn't have any of his pictures, because all his work was commissioned and therefore sold. 'Well, that's it, then,' said our friend. 'He must have painted ladies on horseback. A real horse wouldn't have stayed still enough during the sittings, so the subject would have sat on the dummy. The rest of the horse would have been painted in later.'*

We had always known Auntie May had been a hoarder, but as we opened box after box of her possessions, it became obvious that the reason there were so many of them was that she had, quite literally, never thrown anything away, ever.

---

* Years later, I found a copy of a letter Auntie May had written (just before she moved) to the BBC's scenery and properties department, offering them the side-saddles in return for a donation to the SJAB: 'If the saddles are of no use, I will take them with me, as part of a display of bygone relics that I hope to have in the attics.'

One box was so light that at first we thought it must be empty, but we found that it contained several hundred paracetamol packets. In each of them, Auntie May had replaced the blister-sheets that had originally held the tablets. On the top of each packet, she had written the date, time and quantity of each dose she had taken. I was about to throw the lot away when it occurred to me to look at those dates and dosages more carefully. She had got through the lot in the last three years. She had taken the maximum dose every day. There were three years of suffering in that box.

Another strange find was a brown paper bag like a little stuffed cushion. When I opened it, I dropped it in horror. It was stuffed with human hair. Later, we found dozens more wedged in between many of the tea chests, packing cases and furniture. My first thought was that this was more than eccentricity, this was madness, but Tony said he wondered whether she had kept it to mix with the wall plaster. We knew that she was a stickler for architectural accuracy, after all, and medieval plasterers did add hair to their mix – but that was horsehair, not human hair. And not dog hair either – we found loads of paper bags filled with that, too. We hated finding them; we found the very feel of them revolting. One day, Tony threw one to me with a grin. I caught it and realised that although it was unusually heavy, it clearly contained hair. I opened it hesitantly to find a long, black, wiry hank with two white streaks in it. I was holding a sporran. Months later I found a sepia photo of a man wearing it.

Another frequent find was an old-fashioned soap-powder packet – Omo, Oxydol, and the like. These, it turned out, were just the right size to contain the scores of matchboxes that Auntie May had filled them with. We came across hundreds of them. Each contained fifty or sixty matchboxes. Many held the original matches, now spent; others held small items ranging from bits of broken pottery to coins, beads and buttons.

There was a sack of paper bags full of milk-bottle tops – thousands of them, all carefully washed and pressed flat. Later, we found a pile of pans and aluminium kettles in the garden, obviously saved for recycling. Each had been used until the bottom had burned through.*

One discovery that held me captivated for hours, and which I returned to frequently, was the stack of old scrapbooks I found in one of the bedrooms. There were dozens of them, all filled with neatly arranged items that seemed to have been chosen just for their prettiness: seed packets, photos of sailing ships, Rupert Bear comic strips cut from newspapers, fruit tin labels, postcards, pieces of coloured wrapping paper . . . They were magpie collections made by someone with a keen eye for design. The earliest of the books dated from Auntie May's teenage years – I wondered if she had kept them as ideas for the wallpaper patterns she was then creating.†

There were hundreds of odd editions of the *Times*, the *Telegraph*, the *Daily Express*, the *Daily Mirror*, the *Evening News*, the *New Statesman*, *Tribune*, *Daltons Weekly*, the *Daily Herald*, the *Daily Mail*, the *Hertfordshire Mercury*, the *Eastern Daily Press*, the *Dereham and Fakenham Times* and the *Lynn News and Advertiser*. Most of them appeared to have no particular significance: they are clearly just papers she happened to buy on a particular day. But she bought some on special occasions, too. Browsing through one box, I found the 4am edition of the *Daily Mail* of Thursday, 7 February 1952:

---

* Later still, we gathered all this scrap metal together, along with the aluminium panels of the caravan, and donated it to Guide Dogs for the Blind, a charity Auntie May supported throughout her life. It raised enough to buy and train a dog.

† Alas, the collection of scrapbooks was stolen in a break-in a couple of years after I found them.

THE QUEEN FLYING HOME

The King to Lie in State for Seven Days in Westminster Hall

VALET FOUND HIM DEAD IN BED AT 7.15 A.M.

Premier Broadcasts Tonight After Meeting
Royal Party at Airport

Turning the pages was like going back in time. The story was full of touching details that reflected the shock felt by the nation, by the Commonwealth and by the young princess who was to become Queen.

> The princess had spent some of the happiest hours of her visit at Treetops during the night, watching the wild game by the light of the moon.
>
> Before breakfast this morning she sat writing letters and when she had finished she joined the rest of the party. She talked about her father a great deal during breakfast and seemed particularly happy.
>
> She told Colonel Sherbroke Walker how well her father had looked lately and how much stronger he was getting, and said he had been shooting and enjoying himself.
>
> When she got back to the lodge one of the household said to her: "You look tired, but you look much better for your rest."
>
> It was about an hour after this that the news was heard.

Further down the same box, another paper from that year caught my eye. It was a copy of the *Daily Express*, dated Thursday, 25

September. In the middle of the top half of the front page is a picture of a woman in a beret being rescued in a boat. The headline reads, 'Miss May, on holiday, drifts in a gale' – it's Auntie May!

RESCUED – WITH HER
DOG AND CAT

HOLIDAYMAKERS in macintoshes, dodging the spray on Westcliff, Essex, esplanade yesterday, saw a 35ft. cabin cruiser bobbing in gale-swept seas.

The anchor had broken. The boat drifted towards a sea wall and threatening breakwater. On deck, Miss May Savidge, of Ware, Herts., having a holiday afloat, shouted and waved. Police were called.

Two men – Mr. Gill Pyke and his son Arthur – launched a small boat, took out a spare anchor and managed to tow the boat to new moorings.

In the picture they are bringing Miss Savidge ashore. Her pet dog and cat were with her.

AND here an officer takes a few notes . . . Miss Savidge, her dog Julie beside her, takes tea . . . and Twinkle the cat? She is in the larger bag.

We found huge bundles of journals that reflected Auntie May's curiously wide range of interests: *Flight*, the *Draughtsman*, the *Schoolmaster*, *Radio Constructor*, *Apollo*, Woolworths and ICI house magazines, the weekly newsletter of the Cancer & Polio Research Fund, and the *Journal of the East Hertfordshire Archaeological Society*. There was a foot-high pile of *Rupert the Bear* comic strips cut from the *Daily Express*. There were stacks of special editions, supplements and souvenirs commemorating the great national events that had occurred during Auntie May's lifetime – including all the royal marriages and deaths, the coronation of Queen Elizabeth II, the death of Winston Churchill and the investiture of the Prince of Wales. There was a calendar for every year of her adult life – she had written nothing on any of them, and had not torn off any of the days or months as they had passed.

Squatting in the gloom of that dusty house, I sorted through those piles and found the day of my birth on a 1944 calendar. I felt rather strange, as if I had actually returned somehow to that very year, just for a moment. I suddenly wanted to know what day of the week my sister was born on, eleven years before me. In that dingy corner, peering through May's paraphernalia, I happily lost sight of the enormous task that faced me.

There were hundreds of programmes of plays and films she had seen, and public events she attended, including the British Empire Exhibition of 1924, when she was thirteen, and the Empire Day Festival in Hyde Park in 1929.*

There were folders containing every single letter, flyer and pamphlet put through her letterbox during every national and local election campaign conducted during her adult lifetime. There were hymn sheets and orders of service for religious occasions great and small, including the Thanksgiving for Victory service that marked the end of the Second World War.

And then there was a collection within a collection. Behind a broken-down chaise longue in the kitchen, we found pile after pile of copies of the *Radio Times*, stacked in date order. Auntie May had used them as a filing system: tucked into each issue were the receipts and bills relating to all the purchases she had made during

---

* I later sold most of these to help pay for further renovations of the house.

that week. Among them were thousands of train, bus and trolley bus tickets – some printed on card of gentle shades of pink, green, yellow or blue, and others on flimsy white paper. She even kept notes left for and by the milkman. One scrap of paper carried the message, 'Mrs Savage [*sic*]. Sorry only one blue top. I broke the bottle on the way round and I don't carry any extra. Sorry for any inconvenience.'

There were trunks containing neatly stacked chocolate boxes, their contents consumed but each individual frilled paper case and smoothed-out silver paper put back in its place. There were hundreds of carefully flattened and folded paper bags, plain and fancy. Many of them were printed with advertisements for Fyffes or Geest bananas; some had historic interest (though I don't think this is why Auntie May kept them). Several carried pictures of the Queen or her coat of arms, marking her coronation. Some carried the names of department stores that have long ceased to exist – Bourne & Hollingsworth, Swan & Edgar, Derry & Toms; some were plain; and some carried a carefully pencilled note describing what they once contained: '<u>LOAF. 9.11.90</u>'.

May seemed to have kept all the packaging that anything she ever bought came in. We found flattened PG Tips tea boxes on which she had written notes and shopping lists; we found packets that had contained Austin's Cloudy Ammonia ('For the bath, the addition of three tablespoonfuls acts as an invigorating and refreshing tonic') on the back of which she had written drafts of her domestic accounts. We found the packets of all the medicines she had ever taken, filed after she had finished them between the appropriate pages of the *Radio Times*.

There were neatly slit breakfast cereal and 'mansize' tissue boxes flattened and used as filing folders; there were hundreds of Kit Kat wrappers and hundreds more dog-food can labels, all ironed flat for use as note paper, clipped together with clothes pegs to form little booklets. Many of the labels had carefully written memos or shopping lists on the back. From the dates on the notes and the old-fashioned design of the labels and packaging, it was clear to us that Auntie May had been reusing things for decades before recycling became fashionable. But we also found stuff that had no imaginable further use, including scores of cellophane Cambridge Stocking packets, and various instruction leaflets printed on both sides. One box that Tony picked up jingled as he moved it. When he opened the lid, he found it contained scores of empty medicine bottles. Most of them had contained J Collis Browne's Mixture, the Victorian cure-all for tickly coughs and upset stomachs.

We found all this stuff and more on our first couple of visits.

Then, one day, I opened a box to find that it contained copies of all the letters Auntie May had ever received. She had filed them carefully according to the name of the correspondent, and stored them in yellow folders, arranged alphabetically. There were about fifty of them, and most of them contained scores of letters in date order, each in its original envelope.* There were postcards, too. The earliest of them dated back to the 1920s, when Auntie May was a teenager. I had always thought of Auntie May as a lonely, private person, but all these letters showed that she had made – and kept – lots of friends. In the same box were dozens of similar files – labelled 'Christmas' or 'Birthday' followed by the year. They contained all the greetings cards she had received. I picked out one of the letter folders at random. It was labelled 'NELLIE ADAMS (MRS)'. It contained several hundred letters and postcards from Auntie May's older sister. It fell open at a letter written with a

* Many of the stamps on them turned out to be valuable. We sold these to help fund the building project.

fountain pen in careful, old-fashioned longhand. It was dated 19 September 1945.

> *Dear May,*
>
> *Thanks for your letter telling me about your "Formosa". It really sounds a very nice boat and I do feel most interested in it and shall be very pleased to hear some more particulars when you have time to write again, such as sanitation, heating and cooking etc . . . I do hope you will be moored near some other people as I don't like to think of you all alone on it, specially wintertime . . . if you found it was too damp and dreary to spend every winter on it you could perhaps go into digs of some sort for the worst months . . .*
>
> *Love from Nellie*
>
> *P.S. Has it got a lav? Or what do you do about it?*

I could hear Nellie's voice as I read it. There was a particular tone she adopted when speaking to her younger sister: it was kindly, concerned, and just a little disapproving.

I wondered where Auntie May had kept copies of her half of these exchanges: if she had kept useless ephemera such as bus tickets and shopping lists, she must have kept copies of the letters she had written. I found them almost immediately, because they, too, were in boxes near her desk. There were thousands of them, all filed under date. I pulled several out and read them. Pulling out one at random now, I find a typed carbon copy dated 3 February 1964 and sent from 1 Monkey Row.

> *Dear Marion,*
>
> *Sorry to hear you had been ill again . . . sorry not to have written sooner . . . thank you for all your presents . . . Poor old Moxy, my stray puss, has had to be put to sleep . . . how are your pets?*

And then a charming little reference to Auntie May's charitable work with the elderly and sick:

One old soul, who I visit for St. John and the Old People's Welfare Assn. got it into her head, just after Christmas, that she still had to do 'black out', and in climbing up to fix a thick curtain, fell, and is still in bed, so I have had to spend a good deal more time there than I usually do. It is pathetic the way some of these old people battle along on their own.

•

Going through Auntie May's things was fascinating, but it was taking up a lot of time. Summer was dribbling away and the days were getting shorter, and all we seemed to have achieved was to move Auntie May's junk around from one place to another, creating temporary little spaces in which to work. Tony was scornful of her hoardings – he wanted them out of the way so that we could get the building and decorating finished as quickly as possible. We weren't making anything like enough progress and we weren't going to, until all those boxes were out of the way. But we couldn't just dump them.

We wondered what on earth we could do to speed things up. In desperation, I thought about writing to the BBC to offer the job to the *Challenge Anneka* programme, in which the presenter, Anneka Rice, took on all sorts of seemingly impossible tasks. But before I could do so, Tony had a better idea. If I gave up my teaching job, I could move up to Wells permanently, sort through May's boxes, throw out any junk, identify anything that had any value, and sell it. He reckoned doing this might raise as much money as I had been earning – maybe more – and it would get

May's stuff out of the way so that we could finish work on the building. It seemed the perfect solution. I handed in my notice at the school. My colleagues gave me a cordless electric screwdriver as a leaving present.

I moved to Wells in the summer holiday and began in earnest. The plan was to spend half the time sorting through boxes, and half the time getting on with light building work. Tony would do the heavier stuff at the weekends.

It was a good plan, but I just couldn't stick to it. I found the boxes too tempting and spent far more time rummaging than painting or plastering. My good intentions were derailed almost immediately, when I opened a box that was under the table at which she ate her meals, near the chair in which she sat and slept. (We had worked out some time ago that she couldn't ever have slept in her bed. The space upstairs that she had never got round to building walls for did have a bed in it, but it was covered with boxes that were piled up as high as the ceiling.) The box contained more boxes — twenty-six of them. Most had originally contained Cadbury's Marvel milk powder; a couple of them had once held Norfolk House Brazilian blend instant coffee; one was an old 2lb ICI washing soda crystals box. They were all roughly the same size. Their top flaps had been neatly cut off — later, I was to find them with notes or shopping lists written on them — and each box was filled with twenty or so little notebooks from which the outside covers had been removed.

I pulled out one of the Marvel boxes at random and fished out one of the books. It was ruled for cash accounting but had been used as a diary. At the top of the first page was the number '393'. The first entry read '<u>TU: 23.6.87</u> <u>Cont</u>ᵈ·' Under it, in Auntie May's neat, tiny handwriting, was a list of all her actions that day. She had gone to the post office to post a printed card to Mr Beales (of

Hertford Planning) and another to Councillor P Bellam. Both had been 'filled in on typewriter'. Both cards had been pre-printed (with, I guessed, a message expressing an opinion on some planning matter) by the 'Hertfordshire Restoration Society (61b Ware High Street)'. Each had been sent by first-class mail, at a cost of 18p, which was noted in a cash column on the right of the page under a running balance of £87.45. She had returned via the east side of the Buttlands and arrived home by 4pm. The last entry for the day read 'L.C.', followed by a tick. I didn't know what that meant.

Below this was the entry for 'WED: 24.6.87. MIDSUMMER DAY!!!', under which Auntie May had recorded that she got up at 6.45am, listened to the radio, dozed off again in her chair, 'slept a bit', unlocked the gate at 8am, taken a telephone call at 8.20am, which was a 'wrong number (young woman)'. The milk had arrived at 9.10am. At 3.10pm she had left for an 'optical test' at 3.40pm with Mr Keith Waring, '(partly bald – full beard)', taking with her (as the appointment card required) her 'old specs – 5 pairs', including her 'broken bifocals – 20 yrs old, pair for close work – about 23 yrs old, pair for distances – about 30 yrs old . . . He said my eyes had not altered much.' Having her bifocals made 'will take about two months'. She returned 'across Buttlands' and was 'home by 4.10pm' when she had 'tea'. That day's weather was 'some sun and clouds'. 'L.C.' and the tick are written twice. (I wondered whether it might mean 'exercised Lorraine and the Cats'.)

I could hardly believe it. There were 440 books filled with meticulous records like these. I flicked through the rest of volume 393, and all sorts of details caught my eye. Many were records of medical problems. 'Cut piece of lint – 15″ long – to cover all ulcers'; 'Savlon on inner side of leg, more painful than heel'; 'hot and humid – so sudden – no energy'; 'had to rest R. leg, so could not finish jobs'; 'ankles very tired – too weary'; 'dozed off again in brown chair'; 'left leg again discharging – left knee inclined to bend more than necessary'; 'extraction of L. upper broken tooth'; 'dentist removed 2 more . . . I still have 3 upper teeth.' Poor Auntie May. In all the years I had known her, I had never once heard her complain of ill health; only now could I see how much she had suffered.

But there were all sorts of other things noted, too. She listed everything she ever bought, where she bought it and how much she paid. In volume 393, at least, every list of shopping bought each Friday is almost exactly the same, except in fractions of weight or price. On Friday, 10 July 1987, she got up at 4.40am to find that it had rained a little in the night, though it was sunny and breezy by 9.30am, and warmer and humid by 11am, when she went out. She bought five wholemeal loaves at 54p each from the baker's. She ordered two gallons of paraffin (for £3.20) from Walsinghams. She bought six bananas at 48p per lb at the Yellow Fruit Shop. They weighed 2lb 11½oz. and cost £1.31. She collected the *Fakenham & Wells Times* (18p) and the *Radio Times* (35p) from Martin's, the newsagents. At Howells, the butcher's, she bought a pound of ox liver (46p) and 2lb of pet mince (40p) for the 'pets'. She didn't buy ox heart, which she notes was 68p per lb. (She records a conversation between Mr Howell and two lady customers who are visiting on holiday. The older one said that her daughter in Kent would like to move to Wells.) She bought two 40-watt light bulbs (90p) from Montforts, and a large tube of Savlon from Kinghams (£1.19). In the Station Road post office, she collects two weeks' worth of pension (@ £39.91, totalling £79.82) and meets someone called 'ROS' who has just spent a week's holiday in northern Scotland, touring around and staying in a hotel, which was 'lovely'. Auntie May then went to the high street, and Leftley's, where she bought:

Bananas (ripe) – 42p per lb.	.80
Cup-a-Soup – pkt of 4	.51
Orange cream biscuits (NISA) 300g	.36
Marg – (LOW salt) sunflower – NISA 250g	.24
Peach jam 1lb green	.35
Strawberry jam 1lb green	.35
Tea – NISA 125g	.39
Cheese – 9⅝ oz. Mild Cheddar NISA – 1.29 lb.	.77
Kitekat tins – 400g – 2	.62
Pkt CHUM MIXER (no bags) 700g	.61
Strawberries – LOCAL – punnet – 1lb 2oz	.55

When she got home (at about 1pm, via Green Dragon Lane) she checked her totals and noted that Leftley's had undercharged her by 5p.

Of the 440 numbered volumes in those boxes, the earliest entry is dated 8 November 1946. The last one is Friday, 4 December 1992. How on earth did Auntie May find the time to write them all, and why on earth would she want to in the first place? Why such detail? How could it possibly be of interest that she returned via Green Dragon Lane, or across the Buttlands, or via the east side of it? How can the very order in which she visited the shops be so important that she corrected it with arrows at various points? How could anyone survive on a diet of bread, jam, cheese, biscuits, Cup-a-Soups and bananas? All the shopping lists in later years contain these items and little else.

Standing in the narrow passageway between the piles of boxes, stacks of furniture and heaps of clutter that filled almost every cubic foot in the house, I realised that the answers to these questions were all around me. If I chose to, I could reassemble Auntie May's whole life in the same way that she had reassembled her whole house. I could fit together a detailed picture of everything she had ever done, matching diary entries of bus journeys with the very ticket she had used, finding the packet that had contained the Cup-a-Soup for which she had paid 51p at Leftley's on the morning of Friday, 10 July 1987, and the label from the tin of Lassie dog food for which she had paid 13½p on 22 April 1975.

And then I had a strangely unsettling thought. There was a sense in which Auntie May was still present. The life-force that had once held all those things together, giving them meaning, had not disappeared, but had taken up a fragmented existence in all those boxes, papers, letters, diaries, photographs, newspapers, magazines, shopping lists, jam jars, medicine bottles, clothes, notebooks, bus tickets, invoices, Christmas cards and pieces of whole or broken furniture. A little of the personality of Auntie May, a tiny part of her being, was still in everything she had ever touched and kept. There was something of her in every till receipt and cinema ticket, every Kit Kat label and cornflake packet, every bill left by and note left for the milkman.

It was like a huge jigsaw puzzle, but without the picture on the lid of the box. The picture of Auntie May in my mind turned out to be far simpler than the one that began to emerge as I started sorting through and making sense of all she had kept. I didn't decide to start putting those pieces back together again, I just found myself doing it. And once I had started, I couldn't stop. It was a challenge that I didn't even think about refusing. It was a responsibility that had fallen to me.

CHAPTER FOUR

Distractions and Detective Work

In which I am side-tracked by some puzzling and
unexpected finds

So, during that first week alone in the house, when I was supposed
to be getting on with the plastering, I found myself compulsively
rifling and rummaging. One early find was a folder made from a
flattened cornflake packet, labelled 'Stories to write'. Tucked inside
were about forty scraps of paper and old envelopes on which she
had written the outlines of short stories. She doesn't seem to have
got round to writing the stories themselves – I certainly haven't
found any. The earliest was dated 1962 and the latest, 1983, but
most were written a little before or a little after Auntie May's move
from Hertfordshire to Norfolk. Her imagination seems to have
been operating in overdrive at the time. As I sat at her desk reading
her notes, I found several interesting clues as to how her highly
original mind must have worked.

1.6.1969
<u>*The Fantasy of the Phantoms, OR, The Re-erection of the Wraiths*</u>
How about a story about moving an old house and the associations

*that go with it? Perhaps some [ghosts] would go with the house &
others stay in the place where it was . . .*

30.9.71
*There may be a note of this on some other scrap of paper – I've thought
about it before, anyway. After decimalisation of currency – what about
decimalising the clocks – 100 hour day(?) – 100 minutes to the hour,
anyway – just now, seeing . . . 2 minutes 50 seconds, I automatically
thought of 2½ minutes – due to decimal currency!*

2.10.71
*This one should point out that some of the lonely folks (old or
otherwise) wait for someone to call on them (or do things for them)
instead of making an effort themselves . . .*

4.10.71
*An interesting story could be worked out from the flashes when one
feels one has "been there before" – I think there is a word* [for this] –
I think some people put it down to reincarnation – but suppose it was
passed on by one's parents – an <u>inherited memory</u> which only discloses
bits of itself when something stimulates it to do so – or perhaps only
some persons have it (or have little "flashes") – it might be in all of
us, like all the other things we inherit (looks, ability, etc.) – if only
we could get at it. A character in the story could have a much greater
than usual number of "flashes" – something triggers them off (could
also occur in dreams) – but always they are "memories" passed down
from parents – things that they actually knew about & perhaps their
desires to know what was kept secret from them – this could stir a
character to know what was hidden from some ancestor – not*

---

* *Déjà vu.*

necessarily very far back. The way family likenesses are passed on makes one feel that the memories <u>could</u> be there, to be tapped, if one knew how – take the likeness of Mark's eldest daughter to Alan and Uncle Will & the two cousins born in Australia (Uncle Ben's) – the little girl reminded me of Grandma as soon as I saw the photo, years ago – she might have hidden, untapped memories of <u>England</u> – that could lead to another interesting part – when one goes to a strange town & one feels one has been there before, is it possible that one of one's ancestors had been there? – not too long ago, as towns often change.

<u>This theme has possibilities</u> – someone who feels she has "been to some place before", but that it was a bit different – thinks she may have been there as a small child, but finds that the "difference" occurred before that and that her Mother or Grandmother had been there before it happened – not an item that one might see on a local view card – or if it is, she finds that she automatically knows something about it that is <u>not</u> in any picture.

4.3.72
Write a funny (or light-hearted) story in opposition to the outlook on spinsters – that they are objects to be pitied – no-one wanted to marry them – they have "missed out" on life – they are lesser mortals than the girls & women who did get married . . . <u>Spinsters need some sort of status, not just as "maiden aunts".</u>

Many other things I found were quite puzzling. Browsing through Auntie May's piles of the *Radio Times*, I found dozens of scraps of paper on which she had written odd little notes. They didn't seem to make much sense at first:

'*Could you hear the singing yesterday?*'; '*The dresses were pretty,*

weren't they?'; 'WE USED TO MAKE PAPER FLOWERS FOR
THE CHILDREN, FOR THE SCHOOL PLAY'; 'WE TIED
THEM ON TO TWIGS'; 'Mrs NEWBOULD, who looked after
the HANDICRAFTS EXHIBITION'.

At first, I wondered whether Auntie May's obsessive orderliness
had extended to planning what she was going to say in advance –
she surely can't have written notes to prompt herself?

Then it dawned on me. Many of the notes were in unjoined-up
writing, or in block capitals. They had been written clearly so that
they could be read by someone with poor eyesight:

'I CAN HEAR THE BATTERY NOISE'; 'IF YOU PRETEND
YOU CAN HEAR, YOU MAY SAY YES WHEN YOU MEAN
<u>NO</u>.'; 'You are better off, because a deaf-aid does help you.'

They were her half of conversations she had had with the old
people she had visited who were deaf. She had written them so that
they could read what they couldn't hear. And I could hear them
now: chatty, kindly, encouraging, reassuring. It didn't take much
imagination to guess the unrecorded sides of the conversations,
too:

'Another young man I know is now so deaf that a deaf-aid
cannot help him.'

'Oh, really? How does he manage?'

'He has to lip-read.'

'What do you mean, "lip-read"?'

'He has to look at people's lips.'

'I feel very cold today.'

'Put your wool scarf on.'

Later, I was to find other pieces of that corner of the jigsaw.

One was a little coloured engraving in a Hogarth frame with the title: 'The Priory, Ware, Hertfordshire'. With all the moving of boxes and furniture going on, I thought I had better take it down in case it got knocked off its nail. On the back was written 'Presented to Miss May Savidge by Ware Old People's Welfare Association in recognition of services to the elderly, May 1970.' Later still, when I had time to go through all those diaries, I could see that it was a gift that Auntie May had thoroughly deserved.

When Tony came up to join me at the end of the first week, he looked around, saw how little work I had done and sighed deeply. I can't say I blame him. He had telephoned to ask how I had been getting on and I had lied about how much plastering I had done. I hadn't dared admit that I had spent most of the time losing myself among Auntie May's memories. On the Friday, I rushed to do as much as I could before he arrived, but it must have been obvious that I hadn't done a week's work.

He wasn't best pleased. He said that I seemed more interested in what he called 'her junk' than in honouring my promise of finishing the building. Even as I was denying it, I knew that he was right. He reminded me that until we dealt with the contents we couldn't possibly deal with the house. Even if some of her things were valuable, there was more value in having them out of the way. The best thing we could do would be to drag them all out into the garden and set fire to them – no, he had a better idea: we should set fire to them where they were, and get rid of the whole house, too. He had never wanted it in the first place.

I knew why he was upset. Auntie May's house and property had taken over his life, my life and our joint lives, totally. He had already told me several times that I was turning into her and that it wasn't healthy. I had taken early retirement to devote myself to the project Auntie May had bequeathed to us, but I had been side-tracked. I wasn't pulling my weight with the building work and I wasn't turning up things that could be sold.

To demonstrate his point, Tony picked up one of the boxes I had been going through, carried it out into the garden, and tipped its contents onto the heap of rubbish that was destined for the bonfire. 'No, not that one!' I cried – though I am sure I would have said the same of whichever box he had taken. This, though, did indeed contain something remarkable: one of the items that Auntie May had listed as left to Tony in her will. It was the prototype of a musical instrument that Auntie May had invented. She had called it the 'Selectatune'. It was a cross between a music box and a zither. Its purpose was 'to provide amusement combined with occupa-tional therapy' and 'a means of training the ear in cases of tone deafness and speech therapy'. It was a flat plywood sounding board with strings that had sliding bridges that could be set out to play a predetermined tune, using a plectrum. The original drawings and design notes were also in the box.

The Selectatune and its documents lay on the rubbish heap for weeks, daring me to rescue them. Then one day, I came home to find that Tony had lit a bonfire. The Selectatune was gone, but the wind had blown the scorched papers into the hedge. I took them into the house and hid them under the cupboard in the kitchen, where Tony wouldn't find them.

CHAPTER FIVE

Discoveries of Value

In which I sell some very ordinary things for a lot of
money and part with something very special for
much less than it is worth

Tony was right. We needed to sort out what could be sold to pay
for building materials. If we didn't, the project would grind to a
halt. I got a man from Sotheby's to come in and look at the
furniture, but he said there wasn't much of any value apart from the
upturned chaise longue in the old parlour and a couple of ancient
cupboards. But he did point out something that hadn't occurred to
me: that though all those ancient bus tickets, chocolate boxes and
magazines might look like junk, there were collectors willing to
pay very good money for them. He said the best way to meet them
was to join the Ephemera Society, so he gave me the address.

Just before the Sotheby's man's visit, I had found Auntie May's
Marks & Spencer boxes and decided to find out what they might be
worth. She had worked for the company in the late 1920s and –
needless to say – she had kept every piece of paper that had come
her way.

I telephoned Marks & Spencer's head office and asked if they
had an archivist: they did, and she was called Angela Burns. When
I told her that Auntie May had worked for M&S in the 1930s, she

didn't seem particularly interested – until I mentioned that I had some early numbers of the company's magazine. 'Oh yes,' she said, 'they go back to 1937.' 'But I have got volume one, number one,' I replied, 'and it's dated 1934.' There was a silence and then she asked whether I'd care to come up to London and join her for dinner. I did, and we became friends. It turned out that the magazines Auntie May had left were issues that had been produced unofficially, before the project had been adopted by the management. They were very rare – in fact, no one in the M&S archives department had known of their existence – and they were potentially very valuable.

Angela came to Wells to look through Auntie May's M&S memorabilia – and I sold a box full of company pattern books, price lists and product catalogues directly to the Marks & Spencer museum. I asked her what I should do about valuing Auntie May's other bits and pieces and she, too, suggested I join the Ephemera Society, of which she was a member. So I did. At one of its meetings, I met the collector Robert Opie, who had founded the Museum of Brands, Advertising and Packaging, which is now housed in Notting Hill. He bought a number of old toothpaste tins, Kit Kat wrappers and other bits and pieces of old packaging that I had very nearly thrown away. He was a good man and paid me well for them – he was intrigued by the myriad saved chocolate wrappers, for they had the date she had bought them written on the back. I also got an excellent price for Auntie May's bus tickets. She had kept every one she'd ever bought and filed them between the pages of the *Radio Times* that carried the date on which she used them.

Not everyone I met was quite so generous. When I told one collector about my struggle to sort out Auntie May's stuff, she insisted on coming back to help me value it. She spent a whole day with me, estimating values and putting aside things that might get a good price. By tea time, we were both exhausted, and I offered to pay her for her efforts. At first, she refused to accept anything but, when I insisted, she said something she had seen caught her fancy – and it would be reward enough to be allowed to buy it from me. It was the little photograph of Queen Victoria that had been left to Auntie May by her own maiden aunt, Alice May Savidge, after whom she had been named. It was a pretty little picture, in which the Queen is holding a fan – and was taken by William Downey, who was, I later discovered, a much sought-after nineteenth-century photographer. Alice May Savidge had been employed by him to paint colour on his black and white prints. On the back of it, the Queen's equerry had written a note to Downey himself, instructing him to make a coloured copy and to be particularly careful of the colouring of the chin.

'It's not so much the picture that I like, as the mounting,' said my new friend. 'I know it's a bit quaint, but I think it's rather pretty.' I felt torn: I was truly grateful for all the help I'd had, but I didn't really want to part with something that Auntie May had kept as a family treasure. She told me it was worth about £30, and she'd be happy to buy it for that. I gave in and sold it to her. A few months later, I heard on the radio that it had been auctioned for a sum that would have paid for a builder to finish the work on the house twice over. I felt physically sick.

•

But – as far as I know any way – that photo was the only thing of Auntie May's that I sold badly. I started to develop an eye for things that had no sentimental value and that collectors might want.

A steady trickle of money was coming in and we spent it all on the house. Soon, we had finished the main bedroom, the scullery, the loos and the bathroom, though the rest of the place was still a cross between a junkyard and a building site. The house was still raked by draughts. Most of the windows were still unglazed, their frames covered with plastic sheeting. The house was cold. I had managed to get Auntie May's Rayburn to work, but the only way to get any real heat out of it was to build the fire up so far that the water boiled in the tank, so I had to leave the taps running while I cooked. The house was impossible to clean. Where there wasn't dust, there was mould. When it rained, water ran down the inside of the windows and, at times, it would drive straight through the walls.

Worse still, when the wind was in the north, the whole building swayed like a ship in a storm. The plastic that covered the windows flapped and snapped like sails. The house timbers – which were only held together with oak pegs – shrieked and graunched as they rubbed against each other. The movement would start erratically, gather momentum and then reach a resonant frequency that you could feel in your bones. Then the wind would ease, the vibration would stop and the whole house would shudder to a halt.

The first time this happened I was terrified. It was during the week, so I was alone in the house. I was so frightened the place would collapse that I hid under the bed. It happened again one weekend while Tony was there. We were woken in the middle of the night. He couldn't stop the swaying, but he did manage to lessen the noise. He went round the house with a lighted candle, pouring wax into the gaps around the pegs and joints in all the beams.

It couldn't have swayed and rocked like that originally, surely? What was wrong? Then we realised. Auntie May had taken great pains to restore the house authentically, but the one detail she had overlooked was the relationship between its design and its site. She had carefully orientated it in the medieval manner, with the solar facing south to catch the sun and the dairy facing north to keep cool. But in Ware, it had stood in a sheltered valley; now, it was on top of a hill and sideways-on to the prevailing wind. The frame would need strengthening. More expense!

CHAPTER SIX

A Surprising Correspondence

In which I find a broken heart wrapped up in a brown paper parcel

I don't think Tony was right when he said I was turning into Auntie May, but I can see that there were certainly some similarities. She had started the rebuild immediately on her retirement and I had retired in order to help finish her task. She had been happy to live surrounded by the clutter she accumulated throughout her lifetime, and I was delighting in that clutter, like a child given free run of a toy shop. She had lived there alone and, for five days of the week, I was living alone there, too. She had captured and stored a lifetime's worth of emotions and, as I unpacked them, her emotions came alive in me.

One afternoon, I found a brown paper parcel buried under some bags and boxes at the very back of the attic. It contained a mounted and framed black and white photograph of a man wearing Elizabethan dress. I could see straight away that it was an actor playing the part of Hamlet. He sits in sombre reflection, looking deep into the dark middle distance. Tucked into the frame were scores of letters in their original envelopes, along with numerous pieces of paper covered in Pittman's shorthand. Sitting on the glass were bundles of documents that included old theatre programmes, newspaper cuttings and a passport issued in 1926 and bearing the name of Mr Denis Elliot Watson, a designer, born Newcastle upon Tyne on 9 September 1881. The passport photo and the Hamlet picture are of the same man.

When I pulled out the letters and began to read them, I was taken aback. They were love letters. Nellie had told me her sister had had a fiancé who had died before the war, but the reality of that relationship had never sunk in. In all the time I had known her, Auntie May had seemed a very solitary, self-sufficient person. I knew that she had had lots of friends and acquaintances, but I had never imagined her capable of anything like intimacy. All the evidence around me pointed to a life filled to overflowing with single-minded busy-ness. The idea that she might have found time even to think of romantic companionship just hadn't occurred to me. But looking through those letters, I could see that she had not become a loner through choice.

I skim-read them with guilty excitement. I had been immersed in Auntie May's life for months and thought I understood her: now I had found a side of her that I would never have imagined. There, spread out before me upon a great sheet of brown paper, were all the mementos of a relationship that had started as a tentative friendship, grown into love and been ended by death. Auntie May had wrapped her broken heart in a parcel, tied it with string and hidden it at the back of the attic.

Who was this designer and Shakespearean actor, and how had Auntie May met him? The expression in the photograph in his passport was as Hamletic as the younger face in the picture in the frame. In each, the eyes seem focused not on things, but on thought. In the passport, a middle-aged man wears a stiff collar and tie, and large, round, wire-rimmed pince-nez spectacles. His backcombed hair is receding. He is not young.

I did a little sum in my head. Auntie May was born in 1911; Denis was born in 1881. He was thirty years her senior. I did another little sum, too. Her copy of the first letter she wrote to him is dated 2 January 1928. She was only sixteen. I found myself wondering whether I ought to be shocked.

I didn't wonder for long. The correspondence begins innocently – and it is Auntie May who initiates it. She writes to thank Mr Watson for passing on her address to a potential new employer. They must have met at Heffer Scott's, the wallpaper design studio at which Auntie May had worked, and for which, I guess, Mr Watson had done work, too. Heffer Scott's was laying off staff – and Auntie May needed a job.

Dear Mr Watson,

Thank you very much for letting Mr P. have my address, so quickly; I am sure it is very kind of you to bother about me, and I thought you might be interested to know what has happened.

The letter is polite, friendly and chatty – but puzzlingly signed, 'I am, yours sincerely, Wendy.' Mr Watson's early letters address her as Wendy, too. He must have given her the nickname before they started writing to each other.

As I sat on the attic floor with all those letters round me, I wondered if the name 'Wendy' had any significance. And then it struck me. He called her Wendy because he saw himself as Peter Pan – the boy who wouldn't grow up. It seemed a rather telling choice of nickname. I guessed he was justifying their friendship by defining it as innocent. But just as there are hints of flirtation between Peter Pan and Wendy in JM Barrie's play and stories, there are flickers of more than friendship in even the early letters between Mr Watson and Auntie May.

For years, they seem to write more often than they meet. Early in the correspondence, Mr Watson gives up his job in the design business and tries to make a living as an actor. I could see from the theatre programmes in the bundle with the love letters that he had already had a lot of amateur experience. His name, often in the form Elliot Watson, is nearly always top of the bill. The earliest programme dates from 1916. In 1924, he played Leontes in the Kemble Society's *A Winter's Tale*, which he also produced, and in 1926 he produced and played the title role in the same company's *Henry V* – and produced its *Julius Caesar*, in which he played Marc Antony. By 1928 he has joined the Bensonians, taking the parts of Marcellus and the Player King in *Hamlet* and Gratiano in *The Merchant of Venice*. Each cast includes Sir Frank Benson himself and also Robert Donat, who went on to be a film star and Academy Award-winner. Donat got his film break in 1932 and went on to become a Hollywood star. Denis Elliot Watson was not to be so lucky.

Several cuttings of newspaper reviews were tucked into those old programmes, and criticism of Denis Elliot Watson's performances was mixed. The *Shakespeare Journal*'s review of the Streatham Shakespeare Players' 1926 *Much Ado About Nothing* asserts that D Elliot Watson 'is clearly an actor of great ability . . . But in his boisterous vitality, he overstepped the bounds proper to Benedick.'

Another of the cuttings was from the *Bromley and Kentish Times* of Friday 13 January 1933. Under the headline 'HAMLET – FINE ACTING IN BROMLEY' is a wordy and self-important review full of praise for Watson in the title role. The reviewer found something wonderful, but something imperfect in his performance:

> If the history of play-acting in Bromley should ever come to be written, last Saturday will have a prominent place in the list of memorable occasions.

For on that day one of the finest performances the
town has seen was given at St Mark's Church Hall
in the Kemble Society's production of "Hamlet".

Mr Watson . . . laid on the sombre hues with a sure
touch, until eventually he had composed a picture
only too expressive of all the gloom, the death and
the madness which stalk through the piece with
ominous tread. If occasionally he was carried away
by the feelings of the being he was personating, he
never tore passion to tatters . . .

The following year, Mr Watson is doing his best to get into films,
but he is finding it a struggle.

> *154 Sinclair Road,*
> *West Kensington, W14*
> *5.10.34*
>
> *My dear "Wendy" – You are a most faithful pal – I was most happy
> to have your letter and glad to hear your mother is so much better,
> maybe the new home will be an extra cheer for her – Bless my soul –
> but time does fly and nearly all people driven potty with anxieties or
> something – one d–! thing after another – I have had a hell of a time
> – no work since Jan. but that little bit in "Little Friend". But begin
> next week – nothing to say, just walking on – in "The Dictator" – and
> in about three weeks time have a part with lines in a new film – "Abdul
> The Damned" at Elstree. – I see little of anybody these days – and
> would like to see Griffiths again – as well as yourself – my fault, I
> know, for you have had the patience of Job.*
>
> *. . . Is your hair as beautiful as ever? And do you paint your
> nails – horrible habit – like raw meat! I fear this is a poor letter*

after yours which is so full of interest . . .

My hand is mending – the greatest specialists say it is "mental", caused through worry – well, I have 1/- left – but am trying not to worry – Please Wendy keep this to yourself –

As I am very old – I think I may send my love to you –

Yours ever

Denis Elliot Watson

I couldn't read Auntie May's copy of her reply as it and most subsequent copies were written in shorthand. (I had already found among her other possessions the fifty-words-per-minute certificate she was awarded by the RSA in 1932.) I phoned up a good friend, Jan Paler, who knows Pittman's, and some time later we both sat at the table in the great hall with Auntie May's reply to Mr Watson's letter in front of us. Jan said that the shorthand was 'perfect Pittman's that was easy to decipher' – but as she did so, she wondered whether we really ought to be reading it. We were peeping into other people's private past.

29th Oct 1934

Dear Mr Watson

Thank you very much for your letter which I was very pleased to receive. I am awfully sorry to hear how unlucky you have been and do hope things will brighten up soon. Perhaps these two new parts you mention will lead to something . . .

My mother is keeping fairly well, I'm glad to say. She still has to go to hospital every two months for examination . . .

Wishing you the best of luck and hoping you are both quite well

I am yours

For ever

Wendy

But those two new parts Mr Watson mentioned did not lead to anything and, in the following year, the health of Auntie May's mother deteriorated steadily.

154 Sinclair Road, W14
Oct-23-35

Dear Wendy

I was most pleased to have your letter but most sorry to hear your sad news – I know how devoted you were to your mother and the shock of her passing on must have been hard for you, and being alone, harder still – still, time softens all things, and no doubt you will find new interests in life –

You may be surprised to hear that I have returned to designing – my health would not stand the anxiety of stage work – and I am most certainly much happier and getting my health back – also mother is getting on in years and impossible and not right for her to be left alone so I could not go on tour – I have no regrets about leaving acting for the present anyway – could you come over to tea one Sunday or Saturday – or are you always engaged?* I hope you may be able to meet Mother – just let me know by phone.

With all good wishes, and be of good cheer, Wendy,

Yours ever

Denis Elliot Watson

What a strange man Denis must have been! He seems to have had a kind of emotional blind spot. I wondered whether Auntie May had felt, as I did, that his words of condolence, though sincere, are just a little too brief, and that the sudden change of subject – to himself – is insensitively abrupt.

Either way, the relationship seems to have reached a turning

---

* This seems to suggest that he had asked her several times before and she had said no.

point. Auntie May no longer has her sick, widowed mother to look after – though Mr Watson still has his. He has time to spare, now that he has given up acting. It was nearly eight years since the couple started exchanging letters, and he is actually suggesting they might have some kind of date!

Auntie May clearly hit it off with Mr Watson's mother. Several of the letters to Wendy are from her. They make rather sad reading, though, because they are mostly about how unwell she and her son are.

54 Sinclair Road

W.14

Feb. 19th 1936

My Dear Wendy,

I have been going to write for many days, but I am still ill and unable to go about. Denis is much better although not right yet. He does not forget you, dear, and as soon as I am able, you must come and see me. I feel very weary and tired not being able to walk about. The doctor said I had to be careful and not fall. My heart is the great trouble – and my legs. I will not forget your love and kindness and as soon as I can Denis will fix a day for you to come and see us.

With dear love

Your loving friend

Charlotte Watson

Denis's illness is never given a name, but whatever it is, he seems to suffer from depression, as well. Auntie May writes of her own recurrent medical problem, too – the indigestion that dogged her throughout her life. But the tone of her letters is jolly, uncomplaining and generous.

> *94, Broadhurst Gardens*
> *Hampstead*
> *NW6*
> *1.3.36*

Dear Mrs Watson

Thank you so much for your letter, which I was very pleased to receive. I was sorry to hear that you are still so weak, though I do hope you are progressing more favourably now. The weather is certainly very trying, and doesn't help anyone to feel any better.

Has Mr Watson found time for any designing yet, I wonder?

I am still sticking to my diet, more or less, and am a lot better. The canteen staff at the office look after me fairly well, but sometimes they forget, and on Shrove Tuesday, what <u>do</u> you think they said? They had forgotten the milk pudding, so would I have pancakes? – About the most indigestible thing on earth, I should imagine!

Hoping you will soon be quite well again, and with love,

Yours affectionately

Wendy

The relationship is picking up speed, but there are three people in it, and the pace seems to be being pushed by Mr Watson's mother. The words 'love' and 'affection' are first exchanged between the two ladies. At this point, Denis is writing not as an individual, but on behalf of his mother and himself. He dismisses himself as too old for a romantic relationship with his Wendy, but he – or his mother – has an idea . . .

154 Sinclair Road
W14
April 27-36

My dear Wendy,

    You have been very much in <u>our</u> thoughts of late – and I fear you must think us most negligent – Mother is still far from well and so tired out – in fact I do not know what to do. I may say there is little cooking done, but, that little is more than enough for this ageing man – umph! I am getting greyer and greyer every day – and not gayer. Life seems an awful muddle – and though I am ever so much stronger, am not up to the mark yet. Still drawing and living in hope of something to turn up. Of course, I know there is no help of selling till autumn at the earliest – but I go on – though we have a good woman there always seems to be something for me to do with the house. – which is a d— bothersome thing.

    Now – Wendy, how are <u>you</u> going on – I hope your trouble has passed away, and that taking all things, you have some joy in life – we wish you were nearer to us – do you know anyone who wants a bedroom, etc. – and not much looking after – Mother often says she wishes you were free to come to us – this house is too big . . .

    Do write when you can – Mother is in bed – but knows I am writing to you and sends her deep affection to you – and – if I may – being an old crock – do the same –

    Cheer O

    Yours ever

    Denis Watson

I couldn't help wondering whether old Mrs Watson put him up to writing that letter. I could imagine her saying to him, 'Go on, don't be shy – she's devoted to you!' and his reply: 'Don't be ridiculous, I am 55 years old, for Heaven's sake!'

In any case, it seems to have done the trick. Denis's subsequent letters begin with 'My dearest' or 'My beloved dear' and end with 'love', 'devotion' and 'with a big hug and kiss'. By the summer of 1937, they are clearly much more than 'faithful pals'. It is clear that she doesn't move in with Denis and his mother, as the postal correspondence continues. But the exchanges become more intense and more frequent. And they are overshadowed by Denis's rapidly declining health.

> *154 Sinclair Road*
> *W14*
> *22.7.37*
>
> *My Beloved Dear – Your two letters were a very great joy to me – indeed they kept me going – yes – it is well to write to the office. Ye Gods! How the days fly – you do write mostly excellent and interesting letters – both of which I shall answer more fully on Sunday. – I have had a very hard and difficult week so far and am dead tired out – Mother is very unwell and most difficult – so am I – I fear. Today I was quite done up after a very restless and non-sleeping night . . . I came home with a crawling walk at 5 p.m. Tomorrow though I have a very full programme. Being weary and hot and rather grubby am off to my bath – this will be posted in the morning – though written at 9.45 p.m. 21.7.37 – Eat, eat, eat and be well, my <u>bonny</u> dear – not boney – Bless you, sweetheart*
>
> *With devotion and love*
> *Denis*
> *Do excuse scribble.*

Four days later, Denis writes: 'Life seems a terrible muddle and I feel the lack of body strength. This weakness is most bothersome.'

I can't quote May's replies to these and Denis's later letters, because I can't now find them. Somehow, in all the sorting and sifting of all the hundreds of thousands of pieces of paper that May left behind her, those originals and their longhand transcriptions have come adrift. The irony is as painful as it is obvious: I can reconstruct Auntie May's life in even the most trivial detail, but when it comes to the most intimate and revealing things she ever wrote, the record is now blank. Perhaps it is meant to be.

At some point after October 1937, the letters stop, but then there are lots of short, undated notes written by Denis:

> *Dearest — It has not been my lot to have my supper put out for me for ever so long. Bless your dear heart and thought — sleep, my beloved, sleep.*
> *Denis.*

I sat there wondering why letters sent through the post had been replaced by notes without a date or a sender's address. Perhaps Auntie May moved into 154 Sinclair Road. If she did, she had a room to herself. One little note says: 'Sleep well, my dearest. Denis XXXX'. You don't leave notes like that to anyone sharing your bed.

Another note shows that Denis is doing freelance design work at home again — and that he isn't always finding it easy:

> *My Dearest —*
> *Have gone out for a look about — Drawing very slow this day —*
> *Your devoted*
> *Denis*

Then there is a note that says he has gone out for a walk to clear a 'd— awful headache', and one that is evidence of a row:

Dearest –

There will be <u>NO</u> more bursts of temper – I am thoroughly ashamed of myself – I have to begin all over again.

Denis

I had no way of working out what caused that particular outburst, but I found another note that seems to be an explanation following another argument. Denis had made another attempt to get back into professional acting and had failed:

Beloved – I may be very badly bent – very badly – but not yet smashed – the fault is mine – there is little use in going back over the past.

That I am disappointed about Victoria Regina*is most true – but – I am still with a somewhat curious faith in myself – I will win through –

You are all to me – even if I am no longer a youth – but some wake up late in life – I am one.

Sleep – dear – do sleep

Denis.

Then there is one last letter.

Ward B4 – Bed 17
Hammersmith Hospital
Du Cane Road
26.4.38

My dearest Wendy – Most hearty thanks for your good letter – Dr Davies is a wise man and it is fortunate we have taken his advice which is thoroughly sound. – So far I have had 4 medical exams and two

---

* Denis must have auditioned for the Laurence Housman play first produced in 1937.

blood tests (Do not tell Mother about the blood tests) – and more
exams to come, all by different men – when the X Ray will be I do not
know – and do not be surprised if the knife has to be used. I have no
fear – But to tell Mother would be far from wise.

By the way, send or bring on Sunday my volume of Keats' poems
– in Mother's room I think – if you can find same –

I am very weary today.

Cheer up

All devotion

Denis

Underneath this letter was a plain, unsealed envelope. I opened it.
It contained a folded card printed in Palace Script:

Mrs Charlotte Watson wishes to express her very grateful thanks and
appreciation for your kind thoughts and sympathy, in the passing of
her son, Denis, on 9 June 1938.

154 Sinclair Road,
London W14

•

Auntie May must have inherited the theatre programmes wrapped
up with those letters from Denis – some bore dates before she was
born. Later, I found a box downstairs that contained the
programmes of scores of plays that Denis must have watched rather
than acted in, for his name does not appear in any of the cast lists.
One of them was something that he surely must have treasured –
a souvenir programme of the Jubilee tribute given by the theatrical
and musical professions to Miss Ellen Terry on 12 June 1906. He
would have been 25 when he attended it.

I found lots of other things that must have belonged to Denis, too: photographs, papers, notebooks and working scripts of plays he acted in and directed. I knew that Auntie May had inherited Denis's cigarette box and signet ring, along with his mother's necklace – they are mentioned in Auntie May's will. She left them to her friend Winifred Rozee, 'who knew him almost as long as I did'. But as I carried on opening the boxes that filled Ware Hall-House, I kept coming across other Elliot Watson memorabilia, too. There were trunks filled with Denis's mother's carefully folded and mothballed dresses. There was a signed photograph of a Sir Renny Watson, who must have been a Victorian ancestor. There was a photograph of the grave of 'Ernest Watson, native of Newcastle upon Tyne, Eng., born 11 August 1852, died 8 April 1894: at rest'. The photographic company named on the mounting is Payne, of Monrovia, California. Denis's family must have lived there at some point. I found the plan of the ship on which I guess they returned to England – the SS *Berengaria*. The plan was for the use of second-class passengers – on the way back, at least, the family cannot have been rich.

I realised that with time and detective work, I could find out a lot more about the enigmatic Denis Elliot Watson from the things of his that had fallen into Auntie May's careful possession. What I had found already showed that although they had never been fully united in life, their possessions had been intermingled after his death.

CHAPTER SEVEN

Rebuilding a Biography

In which I start to reconstruct Auntie May's life
using the documents she hoarded and the
diaries that she kept

By the end of 1995, I had opened all the boxes and I knew how
Auntie May had organised her diaries, her papers and her
correspondence. Since then, I have read almost all of them and I am
now able to describe her life in some detail – and show how she
came to be the remarkable woman that she was. The earliest
original documents I found in the archive were some letters written
in the 1870s between Savidges then living in New York. I knew of
these people, for Nellie had told me how the lovely black clock
with the golden lions had come from America as a wedding present
to her mother and father. I also knew that one of her interests had
been family history; in her letters to Tony and me, she had often
mentioned new ancestors she had discovered in various parts of
the world. Looking through her letters to other family members, I
saw that she had exchanged information about family history with
them, too, and I found a folder made from a cut and flattened
mansize tissue box in which she had kept extra copies of these
letters and associated notes. With them was a photocopy of letters
patent dated 13 July 1862 signed by Leopold, King of the Belgians,

appointing Johannes Kikkert an honorary vice-consul in Texel, Vlieland and Terschelling.

Nellie had told me that their great grandfather, Johannes Ludovicus Kikkert, had been mayor of the Frisian island of Texel in the 1850s. At that time, the coastline was plagued by wreckers. Johannes knew that if Texel had a lighthouse, ships couldn't be lured onto its rocks. But building lighthouses costs money, and Texel didn't have any. So he wrote to all the kings and queens of the countries whose ships were being plundered, pointing out that it would be in their interest to pay something towards building one. They agreed and the Texel lighthouse was built. That, at least, was how the family version of the story went. I had taken it with a pinch of salt, but I could now see that it was true – and that May hadn't been the first independent-minded person in the family.

Other papers bore out the stories Nellie had told me about their father, another strong character. Frederick Savidge had been a foreman in a metalwork factory in Peckham Rye. During the First World War it had been turned over to munitions production and his job was to supervise the women that worked on the shop floor. The girls must have been fond of him, for they gave him an affectionate nickname – 'Uncle Vidge'. He was the war hero of the family, though he never saw active service. His heroism was shown when the factory ceiling began to collapse under the weight of the machinery set up on the floor above. Nellie told me that her father had rushed into the middle of the room and taken the whole weight of the ceiling on his shoulders until all the girls had scrambled to safety. The strain of it had damaged his heart and led to his early death shortly after the war. Without a husband to provide for her or her daughters, his widow had to give up the family home in Southwark and find cheap lodgings while she looked for work.

I found a folder containing his National Service Volunteer card and the 'scheduled occupation certificate' that was subsequently issued to him, exempting him from military service. With them was a beautiful little handmade card of thanks bearing twenty-three signatures, addressed: 'To Uncle Vidge – a little recompense for your grey hairs.' It is decorated with hand-drawn pictures of artillery shells and the flags of the victorious allies. It must have accompanied the gift they gave to him at the end of the war – the handsome gold pencil holder, which Auntie May inherited and left to Tony in her will. There was also his death certificate, dated 13 May 1921.

The last piece of paper in the folder was a letter from the surgeon that treated him:

KING'S COLLEGE HOSPITAL
DENMARK HILL
LONDON S.E.5
12.vi.21

Dear Mrs Savidge,

    In answer to your letter of the 8th, at the post mortem examination it was found that the heart shewed signs of disease of the muscle and one of the valves was not functioning. The whole organ was much dilated, thus causing the final failure. The other organs shewed the changes such as one would expect after a long illness due to heart disease. I am sorry we were not able to do any more for him than we did – but he did not answer to treatment at all.

    With much sympathy to you in your loss

    Yours very truly,

    C.F.J. Earl

    House Physician

Reading that little letter brought the physical reality of Uncle

Vidge's death horribly to mind. The death certificate records Mrs H Savidge as 'present at the death'. It must have been a terrible time for May, Nellie and their mother. As I sat there, holding those old papers in my hands, I found myself wondering whether this might have been the defining moment of Auntie May's life. For a ten-year-old girl to lose her father must be quite specially distressing – it's a time when many girls and fathers are at their closest. Was it this that led her later to latch on to Mr Watson, a man more than old enough to be her father? Was this first bereavement so traumatic that it set the pattern for the rest of her life? Perhaps. Perhaps it was also the origin of her refusal to give up her home when the council wanted to take it from her, for after the death of her father, the family never again had a permanent home together. It might even explain Auntie May's hoarding. Her home and the most important person in her life were taken from her when she was young and impressionable. Maybe she hung on to everything because she couldn't cope with any more loss. I don't know – but I did find myself wondering. My thoughts turned to her long, doomed love affair with Denis Elliot Watson. I couldn't bear to imagine how much grief she must have suffered when he died, too.

•

I knew that Auntie May's school days had been cut short by poverty,* but only when I found her school books and papers did I realise what a tragedy that had been. She was scholarly by nature.

---

* Both Auntie May and her sister left school at the age of 14. A cousin, a Mr Hampson, helped Nellie find a job with Marks & Spencer. May got herself a job as an assistant in a design studio, working on patterns for wallpapers and silk scarves. During the Depression, when the design business dwindled, Mr Hampson helped May get a job in Marks & Spencer, too.

Her written work is almost perfect in its presentation and most of it achieves top marks. Her domestic science exercise book begins on 23 April 1925 with 'Demonstration 1: Characteristics of a Good Larder and Care of the Meat Safe'. The lesson is recorded in a flawless, childish hand. Subsequent demonstrations are mostly recipes for meals with precise quantities and costings – a pattern that Auntie May followed in the diaries she kept until the end of her life.

On 7 May 1925, she learnt how to prepare a 'dinner for six' consisting of grilled chops and mashed potatoes followed by ginger pudding. The cost was precisely 3s 6d, including '1 gill of treacle' for 3d. The last lesson is 'Demonstration 13', which took place on 16 July 1925, in which she was taught how to make raspberry buns. But that is not the last entry in the book. The rest of it is filled with recipes that Auntie May found in later life, either cut or transcribed from newspapers and magazines. Then, when she ran out of space, Auntie May tucked in other recipes on pieces of scrap paper. Every entry is dated; the latest is 'Christmas 1983' – 58 years after the exercise book was issued. At the back is a section that lists and dates her experimental recipes for 'Wartime Marmalade' between 10 March 1944 and 12 January 1952. She tried it again on 12 January 1972, exactly twenty years later. The yield of each batch is recorded after the ingredients. When I checked the dates, I was amazed to find that she had been making marmalade, biscuits and fudge during the years that she was living in the Blue Lady caravan.

The artwork I found among Auntie May's school books is skilful rather than imaginative. One of her exercises was to trace a picture and then draw a freehand copy beside it. The two girls in flapper dresses are almost indistinguishable. The patterns that she drew in her first job, in Heffer Scott's design studio, are equally precise. She was clearly someone who strove to get things exactly right. I still have many of the watercolours that she drew in her early years and several pretty drawings of birds. Every now and then, during my rummaging, I would have one of those *déjà vu* feelings – none more so than when I unwrapped a newspaper bundle to find a Chinese vase beautifully decorated with a flowery bamboo pattern. I took it out of its box and placed it on the dusty concrete floor of the great hall. Surely, I had seen this vase somewhere before? But I couldn't have – I had just unwrapped it. Later, of course, I realised that it was in one of her pictures, copied to perfection, and filled with lovely pink tulips.

By then, I had come across a second set of Auntie May's diaries. Unlike the 440 cashbooks I had found earlier, these were printed and bound pocket diaries for individual calendar years – thirty-one of them. The earliest of them was dated 1924, when Auntie May was thirteen, but she hadn't yet started her daily diary habit. The only original entries note a handful of birthdays, including her own, although one made in November 1925 was an uncharacter-istically grumpy sentence: 'I seem to spend all my evenings darning and mending clothes.' In 1929, she reused the diary as a cashbook. It doesn't make fascinating reading, but it does give some insights into her life at the time. She buys quite a lot of chocolate, cream buns and peppermints, and she makes several visits to the theatre. She also buys 'films' (at 1s each), 'hypo', 'developer' and 'printing paper'. She has started taking, developing and printing her own photographs – and, of course, she kept them all. One of the albums in which she stuck them is on the table in front of me. There are portraits of family, friends and pets – all the people are smiling and the animals seem to be having fun, too. There are pictures of Auntie May's colleagues at work in the design studio in Berners Street – though there are none of Denis Elliot Watson, with whom she was corresponding tentatively at the time. There are snaps of days out at Hampton Court, Wimbledon Common and St James's Park. All the photos are bright and cheerful and a fair few are significantly overexposed. They all bear dates in 1928 and 1929. They were clearly happy years for Auntie May.

The first year Auntie May used one of these diaries for its original purpose was 1934. Most of the days are blank. All the entries she makes seem to be reminders to meet people at certain times and places. She 'rang up Mr Watson' on Monday, 22 January, when she 'spoke to his mother as he was in Edinburgh', and telephoned again on Saturday, 17 February; the entry for the following Wednesday reads: 'Meet Mr Watson outside Bakerloo Line Station, 5.45', but it has been crossed out and beside it she has written 'Could not come'. She rang him again on Monday, 26 February and on Tuesday, 16 March, but there are no more calls recorded that year – and she has not recorded any calls coming from him. It seems that she was doing the running at this point in the relationship – though he did write to her affectionately in October of that year.

I couldn't find any diaries of any sort for the years 1935, 1936 and 1938. Perhaps there never were any. Perhaps one day they'll turn up. Even after all these years, I am still coming across stuff that I missed the first time round. The 1937 diary is a bit thin, but it does contain details of a holiday Auntie May took in Cromer, on the North Norfolk coast. She writes that it was 'reminiscent of an old Dutch town', and notes the 'sliced stones' used as local building materials. She admired the wild fuchsia and poppies, visited the Cromer lifeboat and saw a wrecked ship at the foot of the cliffs.

I was disappointed not to find Auntie May's 1935 diary, for it was the year of her mother's death. I never did find the copy of the letter she wrote to Mr Watson to tell him of it, the reply to which I had found in the brown paper parcel in the attic. I have not found anything that she ever wrote about it, but I did find something that shows the death affected her deeply. When I was going through the 440 diaries, I came across an entry that at first, I found puzzling. In diary number 164, under 18 September 1968, she writes '33 years'. Under the same date in 1969, she writes '34 years', and so it goes on until the last diary in 1992. I puzzled over these entries for a while before realising their significance. Auntie May was noting the time that had passed since her mother's death. Why she started doing this in 1968, I could only guess – 9 June 1968 had been the thirtieth anniversary of Denis Elliot Watson's death, which she had been recording in the same way since 1966. Perhaps the passing of three decades since then got her thinking about the other losses in her life. I can only guess.

I found a big chocolate box with a ribbon around it that contained dozens of travel brochures dating from 1929 to 1936. Most of them relate to Holland, but there are more adventurous pamphlets, too, including *P&O Cruises in Southern Sunshine* and *Holidays at Sea* arranged by the Free Church Touring Guild. The ones describing early aeroplane holidays have all been sold now, but they were fascinating to read and the pictures of ancient airliner interiors with easy chairs to sit in were totally unlike anything found in aeroplanes today. All these brochures were fascinating, for they offered charming little insights into middle and upper-class holidaymaking at the time. I am sure that Auntie May would have loved to travel on those elegant ocean liners and flown in those early planes – but it was not to be. However, I do know that she travelled to Texel in 1932 with her mother and alone in 1939, because the box contains sets of postcards of places with the dates that she visited them written on the back. The souvenirs that she kept of that second holiday are rather telling. She went alone. She took her bicycle and her camera, and took scores of snaps. The few photographs that include her must have been taken by strangers, as they show her standing with her only travelling companion – her bike. The rest are of churches, dykes, landscapes and ancient buildings, and most have her bicycle in the foreground. But the memento that brought me up short wasn't a souvenir, it was a letter from the Ministry of War, thanking her for the maps, photographs and sketches of the Dutch coastline. On her own, unprompted initiative, Auntie May had spent the holiday she had so long looked forward to contributing to what was soon to be known as the war effort. Auntie May was a patriot.

When war broke out, Auntie May moved with Marks & Spencer to Blackpool, where she carried on with her St John Ambulance work. Two years later, she decided that she wanted to do more for her country.

> *C/o 38, Finsbury Avenue,*
> *Blackpool, S.S.*
> *18.10.41*

The Secretary,
Ministry of Aircraft Production, Recruitment,
Romney House, Westminster, S.W.1.

Dear Sir,

On making enquiries at St. James' Square, for war work, in which drawing would be useful, I was advised to write to you, regarding some secret work. Before taking up my present work (book-keeping) I had five years experience in drawing, painting, tracing, measuring, etc., in a commercial studio, and also attended the Central School of Arts & Crafts, in Southampton Row, for evening instruction.

At present I am in Blackpool in business, my home being in London, but I do not mind where I go, as I am very keen on this kind

*of work. I shall be in London in about three weeks' time, for a long
week-end.*

Hoping to hear favourably from you,
Yours faithfully,
May Savidge

She sent the same letter to the Admiralty, adding that she was
especially interested in anything to do with maps.

The Admiralty replied that there were no vacancies at present,
but that if she wished to be considered for future employment, she
should complete and return a drawing test, which she did. But the
Ministry of Aircraft Production called her in for interview and
offered her a job in the jig-and-tool drawing office of De
Havilland's. She accepted it. She didn't know it then, but she was
to become part of the team that created the Mosquito, a plane of
revolutionary design that would play a significant role in the war
in the air.* Auntie May's contribution was also revolutionary.
Technical drawing was then seen as man's work – she was the only
female 'draughtsman' in the team.

She stayed with De Havilland's for three years after the war.
When she left, her colleagues collected £3.10 as a leaving present
– a significant sum at that time.† They presented it with a charming
letter of farewell, signed by all twenty-eight members of the tool
drawing office. I found it tucked into a February 1948 *Radio Times*.

MISS SAVIDGE,
    WE, THE MEMBERS OF THE TOOL DRAWING

---

* The Mosquito was extremely light – its fuselage was made of wood – and fast. It had two
Rolls-Royce Merlin engines. It was also very versatile – fighter, fighter-bomber, ground
attack and photo-reconnaissance models were produced.
† Relative to average earnings, this is the equivalent of about £280 today.

OFFICE, ON THIS DAY OF FRIDAY, 20TH FEB. 1948, HERE CONVEY OUR HEARTY BEST WISHES FOR YOUR FUTURE . . . LOOKING BACK OVER THE PAST FIVE OR SO YEARS, WE HAVE ADMIRED YOUR COURAGE, NOT ONLY IN THE WAY IN WHICH YOU HAVE HELD YOUR OWN AGAINST OVERWHELMING NUMBERS OF DRAUGHTSMEN, BUT ALSO IN THE MARITIME MANNER IN WHICH YOU HAVE LED THE WAY IN THE DESPERATE HOUSING PROBLEM.

WE HERE TAKE THE OPPORTUNITY IN SAYING "BON VOYAGE" AND TRUST YOU WILL ACCEPT A LITTLE TOKEN BY WHICH YOU WILL REMEMBER US AND WHICH WILL HELP YOU FACE CHEERFULLY YOUR NEW DUTIES.

The following Monday, Auntie May took up her new post with 'DOTS', the Drawing Office Technical Service in Hertford. One of her first tasks was to design a new logo for the firm.[*]

The 'maritime manner' in which Auntie May addressed the post-war housing shortage had been her purchase of an old Thames water bus, the *Formosa*. She paid £150 for it in August 1945, and £5 to have it towed from Bromley Lock to the River Lee at Ware, where she had found a mooring by the Saracen's Head pub,[†] and rented a workshop in which to store the possessions she couldn't fit in the boat. (The pub had a garden which she treated as her own. She sowed it with wild flower seeds, bought by post from seed merchants. She kept the packets, and stuck them in her scrap books.) She paid £85 to Mr WG Hill of the Rye House Boat Service, Hertford, to help convert the *Formosa* into a floating home

---

[*] I found this and dozens of her other drawings for DOTS rolled up in a chest in the attic.

[†] This is the pub in which the famous Great Bed of Ware used to be.

– and she lived on it for over four years. They were not easy or comfortable years and I don't imagine many people – especially women – would have put up with all the difficulties that come with living on a boat. Her diaries and accounts record all the practical problems that arose, and the cost of putting them right. She had a particularly bad year in 1948, when she took the *Formosa* up the Thames for a major overhaul:

> *11.10.48: Formosa left Ware 12 noon*
> *Thurs 14: Formosa keeled over – smashed crockery – up all night clearing up.*
> *Sun 17: Creekside Lock at last (For repairs)*

The *Formosa* file contains a list of all the crockery that was broken. There are thirty-two items on it, including plates, cups, saucers, jugs, a bottle of milk of magnesia and a 2lb jar of marmalade.

In 1949, the workshop that housed her possessions was put up for sale, along with its neighbouring cottage, 1 Monkey Row. The building was semi-derelict, but Auntie May reckoned it was worth buying and doing up. After completing the purchase on 20 September 1947, with a payment of £270, Auntie May immediately arranged for builders to relay the drains and to strip, repair, rebatten and retile the roof. Her first plan was to let the cottage and continue to live on the boat, but she soon realised she had made a terrible mistake.

Her tenants were a Mr and Mrs Miller. They had been introduced by the Hertfordshire Assistance Committee, which I guess must have been a local charity devoted to helping the poor. The Millers moved in on 28 July 1948, and on Saturday, 17 August, Mr Miller came to the *Formosa* with his first week's rent of 15s. It had been due on 4 August. It was a poor start and things rapidly got worse. His early payments were late and erratic, and then they stopped altogether. On Sunday, 26 September, someone broke into the *Formosa* and stole Auntie May's deed box. She suspected the culprit might have been her tenant. By the following May, Mr Miller was twenty weeks behind with his rent. On Saturday, 14 October, Auntie May found that someone had broken into her shed and stolen a pair of riding boots, a standard lamp and an iron. The following Thursday she 'told Mr Miller to go' and telephoned her solicitor to instruct him to give a week's notice to her tenant. On Saturday, 28 May 1949 she wrote: 'Mr M. said he had received the NOTICE.' But getting him to act on it was another matter.

Auntie May's need to get the Millers out was becoming increasingly urgent. It wasn't just that they were dreadful tenants; she needed possession of the cottage so that she could live in it herself. For some time, the *Formosa* had been taking in water and it was now flooding so frequently that it was getting uninhabitable. To begin with, she used first one pump, then two, to get rid of the water; but it got so bad in April 1949 that she had to call the fire brigade. They charged her £6 3s 4½d for the service. She spent most of the Whitsun bank holiday weekend 'looking for the leak', but couldn't find it, and she kept on pumping throughout the summer. Her diary entry for Friday, 9 September reads: 'Home about 9.30. Water partly over floorboards. Pumped for ½ hour then put seats away – got milk etc. Went on pumping – very tired – kept on falling asleep. Finished just after 12 – no tea.' There are many similar entries. On 24 September, it took her an hour and ten minutes to get the water below floorboard level, using both pumps operating at 300 gallons per hour each.

Meanwhile the Millers had simply disappeared, which was bad news, because they hadn't legally vacated the cottage – they had left all their furniture behind.

17.8.1949: Called at Monkey Row – Mr. M still missing. Heard about Mrs Hughes taking out summons against him, for money borrowed . . .

The following day, Auntie May went to the police station to find out if they knew anything of the Millers' whereabouts, and 'heard about them going out playing cards nearly every night – leaving the children, or staying out, or sometimes coming home in a taxi'.

SAT 10.9.49: Called at Monkey Row. Mr M. still away – neighbours said police had been, so I went to Police Stn. They wanted Mrs. M's address, which I gave them. They said that Mrs. M was miles away – not in this county.

SUN 11.9.49: Went to Police Stn. again (twice) as I had heard that Mr. M. had worked his passage to Canada: Police said he had applied for a ration book in NELSON, Lancashire. He had a young woman with him. The Inspector said he would find out if it was an ordinary ration book or just an Emergency Card – and let me know.

SAT 17.9.49: 'Phoned Solicitor told him about Ration Book (in Lancs.) also asked about moving in and letting Mr. M. sue for re- possession – but he said it was dangerous – there are all sorts of things he could sue me for.

SAT 1.10.49: Called at Monkey Row – Mrs Gay said Mrs M. had been seen in Ware??? Also that Police had enquired at MOSS'S about bicycle – stolen? – Called at Police Station – no news. 'Phoned Solicitor – he says case can't proceed until summons served on Mr. M.!!! Why didn't he say this before? – or do something about it – <u>Am to phone again in a few days if I can find out where he is.</u>

I could imagine how Auntie May must have felt at the time – but I didn't have to, because I found her feelings expressed in a note she had filed in one of that summer's *Radio Times*. I am not sure whether she wrote it to clarify her thoughts, or as a reminder of questions to ask her solicitor – either way, she is clearly anxious:

> *Can I get them out – preferably without making an enemy of him – I think he is dangerous – How can I safeguard my furniture in cottage and shed etc.?*
>
> *Cottage let part furnished.*
>
> *11 weeks rent owing 1948 plus 1 week.*
>
> *Tried to sell my wireless set.*
>
> *? boat burglary.*
>
> *Can they get a council house if I want the cottage? – are they on the list?*
>
> *Is the property to come down?*
>
> *How do I stand as regards to compensation?*
>
> *Should I do any more repairs? <u>Wall bulging</u>, etc.*
>
> *Don't want to lose mooring if cottage is coming down.*
>
> *Do I have to refuse rent?*

As if this wasn't enough to worry about, Auntie May was having a terrible time with her motorbike – her old Velocette (the one we had found in pieces at the back of the outbuilding). There are countless references in her diaries to problems with and repairs to the carburettor, the tyres, the spokes, the drive chain, the speedometer drive cable, the compression release and the plugs. She also records ongoing problems with 'Tiny Tim' – a reference I couldn't understand at first, until I later found the Tiny Tim file, in which I discovered that Tiny Tim wasn't a person – it was the brand name of a petrol-powered lighting and power generator. Auntie May was suffering other mechanical problems, too. During the same period, her water pumps kept breaking down and there are many references to promises by electricians to come and repair them. Most of them were not kept.

Another of Auntie May's worries was the fear that her cottage might be scheduled for demolition. The idea seems to have sprung from general rather than particular anxiety, for in those post-war years, quite a lot of old buildings were condemned and pulled down rather than repaired. But Auntie May put such worries behind her when some good news appeared out of the blue:

> *27.10.1949: <u>Mr Miller came back</u> – to see me at boat . . . Mr. M. took what he wanted and made written statement that he was vacating the cottage & stuff left behind was for me in lieu of part of rent.*

She was rid of her dreadful tenants at last. She spent some days clearing up the mess they had left, and made a triumphal entry in capital letters in diary number eighteen on Friday, 11 November 1949:

MOVED INTO No. 1, MONKEY ROW.

The following day, she went to collect her Lotus wireless set, which Mr Miller had taken to be repaired over a year earlier. When the repair man returned it to her, he told her that Mr Miller had offered to sell it to him. It is the last reference to the Millers in Auntie May's diaries.

Auntie May was in her own home on dry land at last and she was determined to make the most of it. She bought herself a Christmas present – a piano, for which she paid £6, plus 10s for delivery. She stayed up until half-past midnight on Christmas Day playing it.

•

Auntie May had no more need for the *Formosa*, and in August 1950 she advertised it for sale in the *Exchange and Mart*:

> **Houseboat** for sale, 60ft. x 10ft. 3in., ex passenger boat, fitted shaft, propeller, rudder, sufficient accommodation for family, partly furnished, lighting plant, full head room, needs slight repairs and painting, lying Ware, Herts. Write for appointment to view, preferably week-ends. Savidge, 1, Monkey Row, Ware, Herts.

She sold it to a Mr Stoddard for £120 the following October, and threw herself wholeheartedly into renovating and decorating the first real home she had lived in since her father had died in 1921.

CHAPTER EIGHT

A Bolt from the Blue

In which Auntie May's peaceful enjoyment of her
home is suddenly threatened

For the next three years, Auntie May lived a life of happy normality. She got a job at ICI and she was good at it. She made technical drawings of exploded views of plastic manufacturing machinery and, in 1952, she won a Certificate of Merit from the British Plastics Federation for designs she submitted for the Worshipful Company of Horners Award. She made new friends at ICI and kept in touch with those she had made earlier in life.

One name that appears pretty frequently in her diaries is an old colleague, Edward Collins. They exchanged telephone calls and visits and on many he was accompanied by his aged and infirm mother, though the even more infirm father stayed at home. They also exchanged letters, postcards and small birthday and Christmas gifts. The earliest letter in the 'Mr EC Collins' file is dated 29 October 1945. There is a separate file for Mrs Collins, who in the first letter, dated 11 January 1944, thanked Auntie May for her Christmas and birthday presents. When I discovered this three-way correspondence, I couldn't help thinking of Auntie May's relationship with Denis Elliot Watson, which was also one in which 'mother came, too'. But the letters between Auntie May and the Collinses are friendly rather than affectionate. In all of them he addressed her as 'Miss Savidge' and signed himself 'Edward C Collins'. They contain little more than small talk – mostly about illnesses, work colleagues and the weather.

Nineteen fifty-one was Festival of Britain year and, in June, Auntie May visited the Festival Gardens in Battersea Park. The following August, she bought a copy of the official book of the festival for two shillings and sixpence. She kept it, of course. At the front of it there is a double-page spread with a picture of the Dome of Discovery, that seems uncannily similar to the Millennium Dome erected half a century later. The 1951 version contained stands devoted to up-to-date scientific discoveries, but there were also displays about discoveries made by Britons in the past, including Sir Francis Drake, Captain Cook and Captain Scott; and most of the other pictures in the book show the nation's historic architecture, including Georgian Bath, medieval Canterbury and Regency Brighton. The section called *The Land and the People* is illustrated with photographs of a modern coal-fired power station, a shipyard and a newly built school – but there are pictures of a village cricket match and a horse-drawn plough at work, too. The chapter on the festival church of St John in Waterloo Road begins in capital letters: 'BRITAIN IS A CHRISTIAN COMMUNITY. The Christian faith is inseparably a part of our history.' The festival celebrated a Britain that was moving confidently forward, while taking the whole of its proud heritage with it. It was a spirit that Auntie May embraced. It was a Britain that Auntie May loved.

The diaries from this time record a lot of hard work repairing and redecorating the cottage. Auntie May spent many days removing old plaster, stripping timber, filling holes with putty and applying several coats of new paint to woodwork. She got a man in to replace the old sink and associated drains, and had a new concrete floor laid in the kitchen. On the Saturday of the Whitsun bank holiday weekend, she bought a ladder, nails for the stair carpet, a putty knife, a long-handled tar brush, some window furniture, four panes of glass (5⅛ft × 7¼in) and '1 pr 3-in. hinges (½ price – rusty)'. It was a working holiday, but I suspect she enjoyed it. She wasn't just repairing a house – she was building a home.

Having a full-time job and a run-down house to repair would be enough to use up any ordinary person's energy, but Auntie May wasn't any ordinary person. She always found time to do a lot of voluntary work for others. Most of this was through the St John Ambulance Brigade. One of many stints of SJAB duty she records about this time is Coronation Day, 2 June 1953, when she got up at 3.30am to catch the 5.06 train to Liverpool Street, spent the day attending the crowds in London, and got back at 7pm.

Nineteen fifty-three was also the year she started working on her music therapy Selectatune invention that I was to find more than forty years later:

Sun 31.5.53: am going to look up old musical instruments in Hertford Library and perhaps British Museum, while on 2½ weeks' holiday, for any with strings of same length and diameter as "Selectatune".

SAT. 13.6.53. Caught 6.43 from Ware to Liv. St. 2.11d walked . . . to Embankment, then to Brit. Museum Music Dept. They showed me some books, and recommended V & A Museum. Went there and spent most of day in V & A Library till about 5 p.m. Also saw flowers from Holland in entrance hall – sent to the Queen.

Auntie May's public spirit showed itself in her frequent donations to charity, which – like everything else she spent or received – are recorded in her diaries. She gave 2s a month to the boy that called to collect donations for cancer research. She sent a £1 postal order (which cost her £1 3d) to the Greek Earthquake Appeal on Saturday, 29 August 1953; on the same date, she sent the same amount to the Westminster Abbey Appeal. There are frequent entries throughout all the diaries noting gifts to medical and human and animal welfare charities – and there are signs that Auntie May was kind to needy individuals she came across, too:

> *FRI 24.4.53: Old man at door again: 6d and box matches.*
> *SAT 25.4.53: Old man came again wanting to do gardening etc. – gave him 1.6d to get to Royston.*

Auntie May also performed her duties to the dead.

> *TUES 8.9.53: Cleared up Denis' grave – weeds – took heavy vase – cast iron – black enamel with white fleck – also some stattii – enquired about having space filled with green chips (semi-transparent).*

Auntie May's generosity also expressed itself in the presents she gave to her friends. Her diary entries for December 1953 are dominated, as usual, by Christmas shopping. On Saturday, 12 December she bought twenty presents, including some '4711' toilet cologne for her sister Nellie, a book (*Elizabeth Our Queen*) for Winnie, *The Observer's Book of Music* for Winnie's daughter Ruby and some Yardley talc for Mrs Collins. A couple of days earlier, she bought forty-two Christmas cards at 2d, and eighteen more at 1½d. The spirit of Christmas was in the air.

Then, on Monday, 14 December comes the bombshell. Auntie
May has underlined every word of the entry:

> *Evening – message from Mr. Lucas – San[itation] Ins[pector]*
> *(through Mrs. Bell) that he wants to inspect cottages on Sat. morning*
> *with view to pulling them all down!*

The post-war rush to eradicate the nation's crumbling housing
stock has reached Auntie May's ancient corner of Hertfordshire.
A shadow has fallen over her cottage. She will never be at ease in
it again.

> *FRI. 1.1.54: Stayed up all night doing jobs in cottage in Case Mr.*
> *Lucas comes on Sat morning. (He didn't.)*
> *SAT. 16.1.54: Still expecting Mr. Lucas (San. Insp.) to come.*
> *SAT. 23.1.54: Mr. Lucas did not come.*
> *SAT. 30.1.54: Mr. Lucas did not come.*
> *SAT. 6.3.54: Mr. Lucas did not come. Mrs. Hunt & Mr. John*
> *Whitefield came about 3.15 and looked all over cottage. – he says it*
> *is Tudor.*
> *FRI. 19.3.54: Up all night – 4th time.*
> *SAT. 20.3.54: Mr. Lucas came at last with Dr. Wildman – Medical*
> *Officer of Health. They said Monkey Row was first on the list of*
> *property to be demolished.*
> *Afternoon – Mr. John Whitfield called & said that this and No. 36 are*
> *scheduled as ancient monuments – section C.*

Her first efforts were directed to making the place as spick and span
as possible, giving the lie to the local authority's claim that the place
was unfit for habitation. Her diaries are full of references to
painting and decorating. On Easter Sunday 1954, she painted the

whole of the front of the cottage with Snowcem. On Saturday, 1 May, she went to a meeting of the East Herts Archaeological Society at the Shire Hall, and heard a Mr Farthing give a talk on 'old property'. There, she met Mr Gordon Moodey, who was to become a champion of her cause, a frequent correspondent and a good friend.

SAT 8.5.54: <u>3.15 pm</u> – Mr G. Moodey and Mrs. Hunt came to inspect cottage . . . Mr. Moodey sketched my window.

SAT 15.5.54: About 12.20 Saturday 15th May, 1954: Mr Peter Locke arrived about 2.50 p.m. and inspected all cottages – said he did not think there was any doubt about its being a Hall-House. About 4.40 a reporter and photographer arrived from Evening News – they stayed another 2 hours! – notified by E. Herts Arch. Soc.

The work of the reporter and the photographer was published in the *Evening News* on Wednesday, 19 May. Auntie May cut it out and filed it. The picture shows her looking businesslike, groomed and surprisingly glamorous. She had not yet become the little old lady that I was to meet in 1966. The caption reads: 'Miss Savidge repairing one of the leaded lights of her cottage. Experts say they were installed in Elizabethan times.'

NOW DREAM
COTTAGE MAY
HAVE TO GO
"Evening News" Reporter

MISS MAY SAVIDGE, a technical illustrator, has
for four years spent most of her spare time restoring

her picturesque centuries-old cottage in Monkey-row, Ware, Herts.

She obtained a license for a builder to repair the roof, but all the rest of the work, including brick-laying, carpentry, re-glazing and stripping plaster from the ceilings and 20 layers of paper from the walls, she has done with her own hands.

Now she has been told that the building may be condemned.

Miss Savidge is not alone, however, in wanting to save the cottage, for the Society for the Protection of Ancient Buildings and East Hertfordshire Archaeological Society are also keenly interested.

While stripping one of the upstairs walls Miss Savidge discovered a six-light medieval window. The huge chimney breast is thought to have been inserted in early Elizabethan times.

Of Great Interest

Mr Peter Locke, who examined the cottage on behalf of the S.P.A.B. said it formed part of a small hall-house of the late 14th or early 15th century.

"Houses of that period had a central hall over which there were no upper floors, and that this was one can be clearly seen by examining the roof timbers," he said. "It is of great interest, because it is one of the smallest houses of this kind to have been found."

A Ware council official said that a number of cottages in Monkey-row were being inspected, but that their fate had not been decided.

Faced with the problem of finding a home when the war ended, Miss Savidge bought a small Thames steamer and converted it into a houseboat.

Mr Moodey also wrote something following his visit and Auntie May filed a copy of this, too:

EXTRACT FROM –

EAST HERTS ARCHAEOLOGICAL
SOCIETY
President: Sir Henry Maunsell Richards, C.B.
Hon. Secretary: Gordon E. Moodey, 27, West Street, Hertford.

No. 4 NEWSLETTER 1954

WARE: A Threatened Hall-House. No. 36 Baldock Street gives an instance of the surprises concealed by commonplace housefronts in our older towns. A long low range at right angles to the street, to which it presents a plastered cottage gable end above a baker's shop, No. 36 has on its south side an open court, charmingly designated Monkey Row. The end of the building farthest from the street is divided off to form a separate dwelling, numbered 1, Monkey Row, now owned by Miss Savidge, who, having had a hint that the whole structure might be condemned, prudently sought the advice of the Society for the Protection of Ancient Buildings. The report of their architect, Mr. Peter Locke, reveals that No. 36 Baldock Street is no less than a fifteenth century Hall-House, of which Miss Savidge occupies the solar wing. Her part of the premises shares the vast brick chimney stack, inserted in the sixteenth century at the solar end of the hall. High in the north wall is a six-light unglazed window, with square mullions diagonally set, and traces of an answering window survive in the opposite wall.

That this rare survival of early domestic architecture should be threatened with demolition is deplorable. A proposal to destroy the fifteenth century brasses in the parish church would cause an outcry, but a house of the same period has no less strong a claim to be preserved.

The battle to save Auntie May's house had begun.

CHAPTER NINE

Battling with Bureaucrats

In which Auntie May goes to great lengths to keep
her house exactly where it is

In a note she wrote before taking part in a television interview
many years later, Auntie May described her fifteen-year battle with
Ware Council as 'years of uncertainty – it was something like
living with an unexploded bomb in the garden, which might go off
at any time'. Her worries are reflected in a number of newspaper
cuttings that she kept. She was by no means the only homeowner
to have a metaphorical bomb dropped on them by a local authority.
There are not many stories of such bombs being defused.

An article in the *Daily Mirror* of 9 July 1954 tells of how a Miss
Kathleen Deering, 'a middle-aged spinster who hates making a
fuss', had had her house compulsorily purchased by Wanstead and
Woodford Borough Council. Her mother had paid £400 for it in
1948 and had spent a further £300 on improvements. The Ministry
of Housing and Local Government ordered that she should be paid
only £10 for it.

An article in the *Daily Express* of 14 September 1954 describes
land-grabbing like this as a nationwide epidemic:

WHEN YOUR HOUSE IS WORTH
<u>NOTHING</u>

Housing Reporter Edward Brett
plots the way of the grabber

PUZZLE: When is your land not your land?
Answer: As soon as a predatory local council casts
eyes on it.

Puzzle: When do you have to wait years to
receive payment for land seized from you?
Answer: When a predatory local council is the
land grabber.

Those two riddles are among hundreds that
emerge from one of the biggest postbags I have ever
had.

Daily Express readers were asked to tell
of land-grabbing by authorities who seem to
know more about the land than about human
beings.

As Housing Reporter I have been reading
hundreds of your letters every day. And a sad story
it is that many of you tell . . .

Waiting for her money . . . is Mrs Kathleen
Keane, of Acton, Middlesex. In 1947, she reports,
the borough council grabbed a house site belonging
to her and worth at that date £300. They offered
£10. For two years she carried on a legal fight until
the district valuer agreed she should receive £300.
So far, *seven years* since her land was grabbed, she
has received nothing.

You can go round the country with my postbag of letters from victims of planning and compulsory purchase and find sore heads and sad hearts all the way.

Intensified land-grabbing since the war has changed the face of Britain faster than people can alter their ways of thinking. Today the greater part of town areas are steadily becoming publicly owned . . .

Here in the post-bag is a letter from Mr. Harry Tanswell, the chairman of Billericay U.D.C. He forwards photo copies of two letters written within the last month.

One is from Billericay Council to the Minister of Housing and Local Government. It asks permission to pay more for land in cases where the price by the district valuer is manifestly unjust. The other letter is the reply from the Ministry. It says, in effect: NO.

Only one of the newspaper stories Auntie May read and kept offered a glimmer of hope. In the *Hertfordshire Mercury* of 28 May 1954, there is a report under the headline 'Demolition Order Quashed by Judge':

A successful appeal against a demolition order issued by Bishop's Stortford Urban Council in pursuance of their policy to improve the new town area was made at Bishop's Stortford County Court on Monday by Mr. John Henry Tawn, the owner of 79, New Town Road. Judge W. Lawson Campbell

quashed the order and awarded costs against the
council.

The first phase of Auntie May's battle to save her home was an
attempt to keep it out of the hands of the land-grabbers
altogether. Her files contain scores of letters to and from the
Society for the Protection of Ancient Buildings, the East
Hertfordshire Archaeological Association, Ware UDC and its
individual councillors, the Ministry of Housing and Local
Government, her solicitor, her MP and national and local
newspapers.

The arguments went back and forth until February 1959,
when Mrs Clarke, the owner of 36 Baldock Street, the other
half of the building, sold it to Ware UDC. The baker's shop that
had occupied the ground floor was closed, never to reopen —
though the tenants who lived upstairs were to stay for two more
years.

The sale came as a disappointment and a surprise to Auntie
May, who had thought that if Mrs Clarke did decide to sell, it would
be to her. Auntie May knew she couldn't save half a hall-house: it
didn't make any sense. But she didn't give up. She wrote to the
council to offer to buy or rent 36 Baldock Street, telling them that
she would repair it and then, if necessary, take it all down and re-
erect it on another site. They replied offering to buy her half,
instead.

Auntie May seems to have regarded this as some sort of turning
point, for in March 1959, she went through her files and records,
and made a list of all the telephone calls made, and all the letters
sent and received in her efforts to save her home since the bomb
had been dropped in December 1953. There are 220 items on it. At
the same time, she made a resolution. She wouldn't allow any more

decisions about her future to be taken behind her back. Henceforth, she would exercise her right to sit in the public gallery of meetings of the local authority. She would make her own record of everything that was said. She would keep one step ahead of the game – and make it obvious to every member of the Ware Urban District Council that she was determined not to let them demolish her house and home.

Auntie May wrote down what was said in shorthand and made a fair copy in a ruled exercise book. It covers all the relevant meetings of the Ware Urban District Council and its planning and finance sub-committees from 1959 to 1965. It shows quite extraordinary dedication. She must have spent hundreds of hours sitting in the public gallery, usually by herself. She was certainly the only member of the public present at the Ware UDC meeting held on 2 December 1959:

> *At the end of the public part of the meeting, the Chairman, Mr. Bowsher, wished everyone a Happy Christmas, including "the public". (Only M.A.S.*)*

Auntie May obviously wasn't allowed to participate in the debates – and it seems strange to read notes written in her handwriting referring to herself by her name in the third person. She frequently records the councillors' decisions to inform her of what she has just heard by writing to her solicitor. She could, however, put pressure on them outside their formal meetings, and she wrote to all new councillors upon their election to make sure they were aware of the facts of her case:

---

* May Alice Savidge!

1, Monkey Row,
Ware, Herts.
28th May, 1961.

Dr. J. E. Moore, New Road, Ware.
Councillor for Ware Urban District.

Dear Sir,

<u>*500 YEAR OLD HALL-HOUSE, COMPRISING*</u>
<u>*No. 1, Monkey Row and 36, Baldock St.,*</u>
<u>*Built as one residence and divided later.*</u>

In case the matter of my cottage or No. 36, Baldock Street comes up at a council meeting, I hope you will not mind my writing to give as brief history of the case so far, (as I have done in the past to other new Councillors), as I am naturally very anxious about it. No. 1, Monkey Row is the rear part of No. 36, Baldock Street, the little bakery, now closed and empty, next door to the Wagon & Horses Public House, which is on the corner of Coronation Road. No. 1, Monkey Row and 36, Baldock Street were built as one house and the timbers run right through, so that what affects one is likely to affect the other. They were built about 500 years ago, as a small Hall-House, and subsequently divided, probably when the chimney stack was put in, at about the time of the first Queen Elizabeth. Some members of the council do not like old buildings, and as well as that, the new Relief Road may come near here. Watton Road is opposite No. 28 and half of No. 30, Baldock St., so a continuation of it would be two-and-a-half houses away, but a really wide sweep of it could include No. 36 and mine, and leave the Waggon & Horses standing alone, with Coronation Road on the other side of it. If this little house is really in the way, I would rather move it and re-erect it, (including the front part, No. 36,) — preferably after I retire in 5 years time, – than see it destroyed. The Council knows this.

To go back a little, – I bought this cottage in 1947, and the Council gave me a permit to have the roof thoroughly repaired. I have done a lot of other repairs as well. In 1953, the Council began to talk about Demolition, and it was only then that I found out how old the building is. A representative from the Society for the Preservation of Ancient Buildings came here, also one from the East Herts Archaeological Society, and one from the Hertfordshire Society, and they all agreed that the house had been built about 500 years ago, as a Hall-House, that is having a central hall with a fire in the middle of the floor, the smoke escaping through a hole in the roof. The large Tudor chimney stack had been inserted later.

In March, 1955, the Council accepted Undertakings not to re-let until improvements had been made and the Undertaking cancelled – though my part of it was not let, really, but owner-occupied. A year later, they accepted my plan for improvements to the kitchen, bathroom, etc., and the work was carried out at the end of the year, at a cost of £200, – rather more than the estimate. About six months later, they began talking again about pulling down my cottage and 36, Baldock St. This was after they had housed the family from No. 34. Several times in the past, I have tried to buy the front part of this house, (No. 36) and eventually the owner said she would come and talk it over, but instead she offered it to the Council, about two years ago, and they bought it. Then they asked me if I would sell them my part. I said I would rather re-erect the whole building; they wanted me to sign another paper, but it did not even mention the front part, so I did not sign it. The great interest of this little house is that it is complete, at present, though some of it needs uncovering.

About 5 years ago, I was asked to form a Nursing Division of the St. John Ambulance Brigade in the town; the Ambulance Division is the oldest in Hertfordshire, but they had never had a Division for the

*men. Three of the Councillors were members of St. John, and I
thought they would think very badly of me if I said I was too busy; of
course, it has taken a lot of my spare time, and that, and the
uncertainty here, have prevented me from doing as much as I could
have done to the cottage. Even so, it is very comfortable, having a
large living room, about 17 ft. by 11 ft.; a bedroom the same size;
small bathroom opening off the bedroom; with electric water heater;
kitchen with modern sink, etc., gas cooker, washing machine, indoor
modern W.C., garden 40 ft. by 12 ft. and a small front garden; also
a useful attic and cupboards.*

*Some very interesting original features of this house have come to
light, as well as the Tudor chimney stack, with its large open hearth,
downstairs, and four-centred arch upstairs; most important being the
undamaged six-light unglazed medieval window, two lights of which
now have Elizabethan diamond leaded glass. An eminent architect
said that this window alone, put the building into the architecturally
important class, as these windows have usually been cut out and
something more modern put in; once cut away, they can never be
replaced, as they are part of the building.*

*If this house does not have to come down, I would like to buy the
front part, or rent it, and do it up, or even just do up the outside; it
would look charming, if properly looked after.*

Hoping for your support,

Yours truly,

May Savidge (Miss)

Looking through Auntie May's records of the sixteen years she
spent with the fate of her home hanging in the balance, I wondered
how she found the time and energy to carry on the fight. All those
meetings, all those letters, all those phone calls, all that lobbying
would have been enough to exhaust any normal individual. And

Auntie May had being making all these efforts in addition to leading what anyone would think a very full and busy life, holding down a full-time job, running a division of the St John Ambulance Brigade, visiting the old and the sick supported by the Ware Old People's Welfare Association, and meeting and corresponding with a wide circle of friends.

She had also found the energy to remember the man she had loved. Denis Elliot Watson had been dead and buried since 1938, but Auntie May's diaries record that she was still visiting and tending his grave. Among her papers were two bills from Chalker and Gamble Ltd, Monumental Masons and Funeral Directors, 're Grave No. D.7.41, Hammersmith Cemetery, Mortlake'. On 5 October 1956, Auntie May paid £2 10s for the earth that covered Denis's grave to be replaced by green stone chips, and on 30 October she paid £4 5s for a marble vase. I am still not sure why she chose to do this now – the date wasn't an anniversary as far as I knew. Or was it? Had they agreed to marry in October 1936? I have found no written record of the date of their engagement. The letters show that by that time, they were very much in love. Was Auntie May trying to draw a line under her grief? Or was it just that she realised that with all the time she was spending battling to save her house, she was too busy to visit Mortlake often enough to keep Denis's grave garden tidy?

And then I discovered two quite extraordinary letters. The first was from Edward Collins, whom Auntie May had met during the war, some fifteen years earlier. The folder that contains his correspondence is full. His letters all begin: 'Dear Miss Savidge'; they are friendly, but not intimate. Except for the last one, which is dated 2 February 1960.

Dear Miss Savidge,

I thought you might like to know how things are getting on with me. As you may guess, I have been very low indeed and did not have any inclination to write. I have, thanks to God, seen my dear cousin Iris in a new and wonderful light, besides her helping me in the things of this world, owing to her having given herself absolutely to the Lord Jesus many years ago, she has been able to show me the error of my ways and I see now that my past interest in spiritualism was nearly my complete downfall. I now have no doubt at all that it is ALL the business of the Devil. Once I turned my back on that it was not so hard to come to Jesus and ask his forgiveness for my sins. I had got to the state that even the smallest one looked so black that I was scared of it and the big ones brought tears to my eyes – this is absolutely the truth. With Iris's prayers and guidance . . . I experienced the wonderful thrill of being born again last Sunday. I did not expect it and doubted it could ever happen to me – I did not see Iris at all last week-end but despite that I experienced the most wonderful day in my life and it still continues. I can only thank the Lord Jesus for what he has done for such a sinner as I was. As you can tell from this I have changed a great deal. I would like to bring Iris over to Ware to see you when you feel like it, she is a very dear person and I know you, too, will love her – everybody does!

I for one cannot love her enough as she certainly saved my soul from eternal damnation by bringing me to the foot of the cross – the Lord then did the rest. However much I feel for her I love my Lord Jesus much, much more – words just fail to express how much or how I feel. I know this will hurt you as I know only too well how you feel towards me, believe me I do appreciate it and do pray to the Lord that you too may experience this most wonderful love. For my part and I am sure that I can write for Iris in this, I should like nothing better than that you be able to regard us as a new sister and brother. You can rest assured that if there is anything that I or we can help you in either a spiritual or a worldly way we would be very happy indeed to do it.

Believe me, knowing what a comfort you were during the days just after the passing of my dear mother, this has been a difficult letter to write and in writing it I have prayed long and earnestly to the Lord.

I do hope that poor Mrs Allen is still keeping in good health – no colds etc. though we know that her passing would be a blessing. I pray that she might find peace and rest. How are the animals, do hope Candy* is calming down a little or she will be too much for you. The "milk bottle tops" are mounting up again and will bring them over some time. I must end here as it's about bed time. I send you all my best wishes and may the Lord bless you and protect you with his most precious love.

Yours sincerely,

Edward A.C.

1, Monkey Row,
Ware, Herts.
18th February, 1960.

Dear Edward,

Please excuse the typing, but I cannot see to write. Thank you for your letter, explaining the situation more fully. I had, of course, realized what was happening, two or three weeks earlier, which was why I stopped 'phoning you.

Am very glad to hear that you have become a Christian. I did not know that you were not one, before; you sounded sincere when you joined in with the Lord's prayer, during the radio Watch Night Service. Your attitude towards Churches, years ago, always struck me as strange; you used to say that we would have to be married in a

---

* Candy was Auntie May's cat.

Registry Office, because you would not go into a Church as they made you feel queer; but then you had so many odd fears – I put them down to your sheltered upbringing. You seemed to have forgotten about it, at your Father's funeral, and your Mother's, and I thought it was probably due to an early recollection of too much incense, and that you had got over it.

Perhaps I took it for granted that you believed in God, because I do and always have done. I have lived without human company for the last twenty-five years, and at times before that, too; through more difficulties and dangers than average; this is a way at living that you know nothing about. I wonder what you think kept me going? I don't think I would be sane now, if I had not been able to talk and pray to God. It is true that I do not talk about it much, but I have been rebutted in the past, when trying to talk seriously to you; once when I had waited for days for a chance to say something, all you said was, "Look, there's one of the new Churchill tanks!"

I knew you had faults, (who has not?) I was not blind – some of them upset me a good deal, but because you had convinced me that you were fond of me and had need of me, I did not criticize unduly; I just hoped to be able to show you, gradually, that life can be lived differently, and I think I had made some progress. Now your Cousin, who you had only met twice in the past, has come along and changed you completely in a few hours. It surprises me, though, that anyone so dear and lovable as your Cousin Iris, should have thought it right to come between us, after seventeen years. It is not as though I am an evil spirit from whom you had to be parted before you could reform; I would not have tried to hold you back. I have not lived a gay life, nor an easy one, and among other things, surely twenty years of St. John Ambulance work is in keeping with the teaching of Jesus Christ, "Inasmuch as you did it unto the least of my brethren, ye did it unto Me". The Order of St. John has two mottoes: "For the Faith" and

"For the Service of Mankind" and our work is carried out without distinction of race, class or creed. But perhaps Iris did not think to ask, and you did not bother to tell her, about my existence. The world would be in a difficult state if all the converted fell in love with the converter, yet you seem to think that what you have done is right; one would think from the way you write that you had given up your girl friend and gone back to your wife.

In your letter you say you know *"only too well"* how I feel towards you, which rather implies that I made the advances, and that you had no feelings towards me. I wonder if you remember how this episode started? When we became acquainted seventeen years ago, I had been alone for nearly eight years;* Denis had been dead for nearly five years, and I had reached a state of peace – not happy, but cheerful and busy; and when you asked me to go out with you, after that car crash, I did not really want to break faith, but then agreed to go as long as it was only in a friendly way – nothing serious. That did not suit you, however; you said you were awake all night, crying, which made me change my mind, because it did not seem right to make you unhappy. Is it surprising that I thought you really cared? During the months that followed, you often spoke of our marriage, – once you said you were glad that I had not married Denis, because your parents would not like you marrying a widow. Then on 22nd August, 1943, you announced that you had remembered that before you met me, you had decided to stay single and look after your parents, and that you still intended to do so, but you did not want them to know why you were staying single. I remember I thought I would still have a friend to turn to, and said so, but soon found out that this was not necessarily so, and during the years that followed, single-handed and often in difficulties, and sometimes in danger, and you, the only one who knew

---

* That is, since her mother's death.

it, not bothering to come and offer a helping hand, I became convinced that you had finished with me completely, and were drifting quietly out of my life; I knew I would never have left you to face alone some of the situations that I had to deal with, and if I had never seen you again, then, I would not have been surprised. But later, you changed again, and became more like your old self, and you spoke as if we still belonged to each other – for instance, when you said you had bought a "Mayflower" car, you said, "Now I have two Mays". Your Mother also changed in the last few years, as if she knew at last, why we had not married; I did not know whether you had told her or whether she had guessed, but she was different, – more gentle and more affectionate, as if trying to say, "I know and I'm grateful".

And now that your Mother has gone and you are free to marry, you have suddenly transferred your affections to someone new, and would like me to be a sister to you and Iris. I am afraid I have had enough. Seventeen years is a long time, and I have put up with a great deal, but there is a limit. It is all right for you – you have had your parents all these years, and now you have Iris you have had me in the background, in case you needed me, and now you do not need me any longer. You have made your choice, and no doubt Iris is much more suitable, – but my heart is not made of stone, and I am not suffering from loss of memory; – in the small hours of the morning, when I am wide awake, I wish I could forget. Still I thank God that we were not married already, if you can change like this. No doubt it is better as it is; you might have wanted me to give up my St. John work, if you had married me, and I expect I can do more good this way. I hope you will be more faithful to Iris than you have been to me.

May God teach you to be patient, tolerant, kind and forgiving towards your fellow human beings who you meet in your everyday life, remembering that they are all His children, as well as you, and equal in His sight, and that any of them may be putting a brave face on a life of difficulty and tragedy, such as you have never known, and that one more harsh word may be the breaking point. May He also teach you not to be afraid, except of His displeasure, and to be faithful.

So I will close the book on our story, which has brought so much more unhappiness than anything else, during its seventeen years.

Good-bye.

'The day returns and brings us the petty round of irritating concerns and duties. Help us to play the man; help us to perform them with laughter and kind faces, let cheerfulness abound with industry. Give us to go blithely on our business all this day, bring us to our resting beds weary and content and undishonoured, and grant us in the end the gift of sleep. Amen.'

R.L.S.*

The Commissionaires at the gatehouse of Murphy Radio, Bessemer Road, Welwyn Garden City, will gladly accept silver paper and milk bottle tops in aid of the Guide Dogs for the Blind; the collector's name is Mr. Lawrence.

How could I have missed it? Auntie May had had a boyfriend – of sorts – for seventeen years, and I hadn't noticed. I went back through the papers and diaries again, but I still couldn't find any signs of it. There were chatty letters, Christmas and birthday cards, diary entries recording visits to this fellow and his parents, but nothing to suggest anything more than friendship. Except one thing, perhaps. In his file was an undated small piece of paper that must have accompanied one of the birthday presents they exchanged. On it, in his distinctive hand, is written '*May 24th 1958: With love and best wishes*' followed by his initials. It is the only other time the word 'love' occurs in any correspondence between them.

---

* Robert Louis Stevenson.

Had they loved each other? I wonder. Auntie May doesn't seem to have found much to admire in Edward except his devotion. When that failed, she saw only faults. It seems that the only time there was any intensity in the relationship was when it ended. Her letter does not express the sorrow of a disappointed lover, but the anger of someone who feels she has been strung along and used. It is the only thing she ever wrote that contains even a trace of self-pity. It is the only time that she expresses any kind of bitterness. It is the only time she mentions the pain of loneliness. And it marks the moment when she realised that she would spend the rest of her life on her own.

CHAPTER TEN

Working Holidays

In which Auntie May prepares for the possibility that
ultimately, the house might have to be moved

By the early 1960s, 1 Monkey Row was becoming increasingly
isolated. Auntie May's home was surrounded by an ever-widening
area of empty, derelict buildings and the spaces where other
buildings had once been. In March and April 1963, numbers 32 and
34 Baldock Street were demolished. The wreckers were almost at
the gate. In June 1963, she received a letter from a Mr Doubleday
of Hertfordshire County Council, letting her know that the
Hertfordshire Buildings Preservation Trust would like to reuse
materials salvaged from 1 Monkey Row and 36 Baldock Street after
they had been demolished. The demolition was not an 'if', but a
'when'. Auntie May was having none of it. She told him what she
had already told the Ware Urban District Council countless times:
that if she was allowed to rent 36 Baldock Street and keep it when
both halves of the medieval hall-house had to be taken down, she
would save the whole building by re-erecting it elsewhere.

But the wheels of local government bureaucracy were turning
slowly. Eighteen months later, 1 Monkey Row was still standing
and Auntie May was still living in it. Some members of the council
now tried a different tack, arguing that the condition of 36 Baldock

Street was so poor as to make it a danger to the public. It had been empty and unmaintained since 1961. But other councillors stood up for Auntie May as her record of the Ware UDC meeting of 7 October 1964 shows.

Ware UDC Meeting   *8 pm, Wednesday, 7 October 1964*

M. Goldstone (chairman); Mr Avery (vice-chairman)
Mrs Cooper; Mr Davenport; Mr Beazley; Mr Murphy; Mr Green; Mr J Sutcliffe.
Absent – Mr Doyle and the surveyor (whose father had just died).

No. 335. 36 Baldock Street.
The condition of this building was discussed when certain members expressed the view that it was a possible danger to the public.

Clr Murphy reminded the members that Miss Savidge, of 1 Monkey Row had asked the council some years ago if she might keep 36 Baldock Street decorated until such time as she retired when she wished to demolish her cottage and 36 Baldock Street and to re-erect the cottage on another site. She was due to retire in 1966.

The building of which 1 Monkey Row formed part was a fifteenth-century hall-house preserving the greater part of an original structure with Elizabethan and later alterations.

It was stated that Miss Savidge had been informed in 1960 that there was a possibility of the relief road affecting her property and advised to arrange as soon as possible the demolition of the property.

It was decided that the Surveyor be asked to inspect the property and report whether in his view 36 Baldock Street was in a condition dangerous to the public, and that the County Council be asked whether in fact the relief road would affect this property.

Only one week before the General Election – some of the Labour
councillors got carried away by party politics.
The meeting closed about 9.15pm.

Demolition day was approaching, but Auntie May still hadn't
found a site on which to re-erect her house. I would have thought
that with so many friends in and around Ware, with all her
charitable work for the local old people's welfare association and
the St John Ambulance Brigade, and with her sister living nearby,
the obvious thing to do would be to rebuild the house locally, but
Auntie May was never one to do the obvious. She saw it as an
opportunity for a fresh start – and she had a hankering to find
somewhere by the sea. It was in her blood. Her grandfather had
been a Norwegian fisherman, and living on the boat had been a
really adventurous part of her life. The two coastlines she knew
and loved were those of the West Country and East Anglia, and she
decided to explore the possibilities of both.

In October 1964, she took a fortnight's holiday in Wells-next-
the-Sea, Norfolk, where she rented a small furnished flat for
six guineas a week. It is clear from her papers, diaries and
correspondence that she planned every aspect of the holiday with
her usual attention to detail. I found the notebook she manufactured to contain the checklist of things she put in her luggage.
She made it by stringing together pieces of lined paper that she
had cut to form alphabetical index tabs. It contains everything
you might expect anyone to take on holiday – and very much
more. The first entry under 'A' is 'address books (3)', and down
between the 'Alarum clock (green one)' and 'Anti-histamine
cream' is 'Alkathene film or bag to sit on if damp (large)'. She
takes her 'Christmas card list', an 'Enamel plate for steaming

fish',* a 'Face flannel' and a 'Foot flannel', a 'Shovel (for D[inkie]'s bucket)', a 'Shoe horn', a 'Tea cosy' and 'Vaseline (for hair) (and Dinkie)'. Under 'K', there is only 'Knitting'; I had half expected to find 'Kitchen sink'.

In July, she had written to the Wells council to ask for a list of places to stay, and had selected West House in Freeman Street, run by a Mrs Groom. Mrs Groom wrote to explain that the last leg of the train service to Wells would cease to operate on 3 October, so Auntie May sent a letter to the divisional manager of British Railways Eastern at Norwich Station to ask how best to complete her journey. He replied that she should travel as far as Dereham and then get the Eastern Counties Omnibus Company bus. Auntie May visited Ware station to find out the cost of the journey, made a list of everything she needed to take with her, arranged for Mrs Crisp at the Hope public house to keep an eye on her cottage, and booked a taxi from Charvill's to take her, her pets and her luggage to the station. On the morning of Saturday, 10 October she cancelled her order for bread and took her document box to the bank for safe keeping. On her way home, she saw a reminder of the destruction that was edging its way closer to her house:

W.U.D.C. men . . . destroying the garden opposite – for 2 p[ai]rs semi-det[ached] houses – Mr. G. had worked on it for 40 years – began before house was finished.

Despite all her careful preparations, Auntie May's holiday did not begin as smoothly as she had planned. It rained heavily the night before she left, so she didn't get her tickets in advance. There

---

* I've still got it!

would have been plenty of time to buy them on the day if the car from Charvill's turned up at noon, as agreed, but it didn't. It was nearly twenty minutes late. Her train was at 12.27, and she had a phenomenal quantity of luggage to get onto it. It had to be held up for her, while the porters heaved it all aboard. Much of it — too much, it would turn out — was piled onto her eccentrically designed pushchair, which had a T-bar for a handle, that made it difficult to steer when overloaded. She had her dog on a lead and her cat in a basket. She had to get all this off and on the train four times during the journey — she had to change at Broxbourne, Bishop's Stortford, Ely and Wymondham. She gave the porters that helped her a total of 7s in tips. When she got off at Dereham, the struggle continued:

Bus driver had no key to boot, so my stuff occupied front seat* — bus left as soon as we were all on.

Arr. Wells about <u>5.45 pm</u> — no car to hire. <u>Dumped us at Stn.</u>: (later 'I heard there are 2 taxis if you know where to 'phone). My pushchair had lost one back tyre on the way, then the front one came off — pushing was very difficult — stuff kept slipping — pavement bad in places (buildings demolished.) A fisherman carried Dinkie as far as a public house. Pushchair made dreadful noise. I had to take Dinkie separately for a few yards, then come back for pushchair with luggage. A lady finally carried Dinkie to the Groom's gate — I would not have known — no name on it — no number. <u>Arr. About 6.45 pm.</u> (1 hour from Stn.!) There is also a drive which is easier than the steps in the garden path. Mr. & Mrs. Groom invited me in for a cup of tea . . . very nice flat — very large bed-sitting

---

* She thus had to buy a ticket for the pushchair. It cost 11d.

room – 20'6" x 16'4" + 2'8" x 7'3" inside fireplace, also kitchen 10'2" x 7'9", larder, etc.

There was 1 pt. of milk I had asked for. Slept till 7 am. (clock struck 3 – wondered why it was light!)

Auntie May appears to have thoroughly enjoyed her fortnight in Wells, though I don't suppose many of Mr and Mrs Groom's guests began their stay by measuring the dimensions of the flat. She explored the town, the harbour, the coastline and the countryside. But she wasn't just here for a holiday. She visited all the local estate agents, and called on the council's surveyor, Mr Rogers and the town clerk, Mr Poynter, to find out whether there would be any problem getting permission to re-erect her house. She got on well with them – 'they both seemed very nice', she writes – and Mr Rogers told her that 'they would give sympathetic consideration' to the idea. Auntie May then viewed several building plots – even though, as she told Mr Rogers, she still 'might not have to move' her house after all. She thought that there was still a chance that it might be spared. Just in case it wasn't, she asked the Wells estate agents to add her name to their mailing lists.

For more than a year after Auntie May returned from her holiday, Ware UDC's plans to demolish 1 Monkey Row and 36 Baldock Street seem to have been on the back burner. Then, in late November 1965, it transferred ownership of 36 Baldock Street to the Hertfordshire County Council. It was a move that brought a demolition order for both properties a step nearer. But Auntie May's retirement date was getting nearer, too. She would soon have the time needed to arrange for the house to be taken down and re-erected elsewhere, if it came to it.

WED. 18.5.66

10.30 am. Research Cnf. Room – my Retirement Presentation
(Dr. Child) Quite a number came – cheque for £9 (+ 7s 6d later) for
me to get binoculars (or telescope) – no time beforehand.

Dr C. said some very nice things – my mind went blank, when I
started, a glance at my notes reminded me – though I can't remember
exactly what I said at first.

The first thing Auntie May did in her retirement was to return to
Norfolk, where she revisited Wells and took another look at some
of the building plots she had first seen in 1964 – but none of them
seemed quite right for her, and in any case, she still felt there was
just a chance that she might not have to move. On her return, her
diary fills with references to SJAB meetings and events, including
a flag day, fundraising sales, fêtes, first aid demonstrations, training
sessions and inspections. But thoughts of moving were never far
away. A note made on Monday 4 July records that she heard on
the radio that a Mrs Topham Smith had 'moved a timber-framed
house 25 miles'.

On Saturday, 30 July 1966, Auntie May attended my wedding
to Tony in All Saints Church, Croxley Green, Hertfordshire.
Immediately afterwards, she started planning a site-hunting
trip to the West Country. Mindful of the trouble she had had
carrying all her luggage on her last holiday, she bought herself
a Portable Porter trolley, with two wheels and webbing straps,
for 7s 6d. On Thursday, 25 August, she went to the railway
station to buy her return ticket to Dartmouth, recording that
she paid £6 3s for it, and £3 2s for Candy, who travelled as
a 'child'. She also recorded the details on her seat reservation
from Paddington to Kingswear, the ticket for which I found

between the appropriate pages of that week's *Radio Times*:

> *N°. M.333406 – for 10.05 train*
> *Coach H. Seat 24.*
> *Facing Engine.*

She tried to book a car to take her to Ware station in time for the 7.27 to London the following Saturday, but found that Charvill's didn't start work until 8am, and Joan's Car Service didn't open before 9am. She'd have to get to the station by bus.

At 7 o'clock in the morning on Saturday, 27 August, Auntie May and Candy set out with her pushchair and Portable Porter, carrying a small cabin trunk, a large blue polythene bag, a leather bag, a zip handbag and a cat basket containing Dinkie. Miss Stewart, a friend of hers, happened to be at the bus stop. She told Auntie May that she wasn't sure that the 7.12 bus still ran – but it did, and the driver/conductor, Mr Flood, helped Auntie May get her luggage on board, while Miss Stewart held Candy's lead. Unfortunately, the dog got overexcited and pulled so hard that the collar clip broke. Auntie May did catch the 7.27, but when she picked up her trunk in order to change at Broxbourne, the handle came off in her hand, and she had to tie it up with the length of rope she had brought to tie things to the pushchair. This turned out to have been a fortunate accident, because when she went to pick up the trunk at Liverpool Street, she saw that the hinge of the lid, which was made only of fabric, had torn from end to end. At Paddington she was told that she would have to buy a return ticket for 11s 3d for the cat; and when she finally got all her stuff onto the 10.05, she found that 'both H.24s had been marked "facing engine" (or had the other one been altered? It looked like it.)'

Once again, Auntie May had made a disastrous start to a

holiday, but once again, there was no mention of annoyance or frustration in the record she made. If I were given to writing diaries, I would certainly have mentioned my anger at a taxi firm that sent a car so late that I nearly missed my train, or at a fellow passenger who had forged a ticket reservation so as to occupy the seat I had booked. I would have been furious to be told half-way through a journey that I had to pay extra for a cat carried in a basket, and I would have made my fury a matter of record. I would have been thoroughly fed up if the handle had come off a piece of luggage, and the lid had all but come off, too, and I would have written up my annoyance as part of my memory of the day. But Auntie May does no such thing. Her records are meticulous to the point of obsessiveness, but there is never any mention of resentment when things went wrong.

Why, I wonder? Is it that she was only interested in recording facts, not feelings? I don't think so. Those 440 diaries contain hundreds of references to how she felt when she was unwell, when she had 'no energy' in hot or humid weather, or when she was 'tired' or 'exhausted' after overdoing it – though her interest was in the fact that she was tired rather than what feeling tired was like. She does, at least occasionally, write up her feelings about people she met or dealt with. She writes of Mr Poynter and Mr Rogers in Wells that they 'both seemed very nice'. She also records sights that she found moving, including this, on her West Country holiday:

TUES 30.8.66 . . . Full moon was rising (from bank of cloud just above the sea horizon) – golden colour – reflected right across to the beach – beautiful sight.

Such glimpses of Auntie May's emotions are rare, but when they do appear, they are nearly always positive. One uncharacteristic expression of annoyance is in an entry for Monday, 12 December 1966, when she describes how another dog savaged Candy in the street while her owner did nothing to intervene:

Fancy bringing out a dog like that, without a lead. She must have known what he was like, by the way she called him in the first place. A dog is supposed to be 'under control'.

I think that one reason Auntie May records so few negative thoughts in her diaries is that she didn't have many. I can honestly say that in all the years I knew her, I never heard her utter a complaint – not even in her awful final illness. She simply accepted her lot and made the best of it. She didn't write up those disasters with the taxis and the luggage and the tickets because they had annoyed her, but because they had happened.

As to why she should want to record her life in such detail at all – well, that's another question. I've spoken to lots of people about her in the years since she died, and I've given lots of talks about her to groups of people, some of whom had known her. Some think she wrote up everything simply because she had a compulsive personality. They give the same explanation for her hoarding. I am sure this must be true, but I don't think it's the whole truth. It doesn't explain why this compulsiveness should show itself in keeping a running record of one's life, or in hanging on to everything that comes into one's hands. Somebody suggested that Auntie May suffered from a condition known as Obsessive Compulsive Disorder, but I am not convinced. Some OCD sufferers are indeed compulsive hoarders, but what I have read about them suggests that their hoarding gets between them and their ability to cope with the world. Auntie May was able to cope with anything. Her diaries are the proof of it. OCD hoarders tend to be loners. Auntie May certainly lived alone, but she had scores of friends and acquaintances – her diaries are full of references to them. No, I don't think she suffered from a mental illness.

I am not a psychiatrist or a psychologist. I can't offer a professional opinion on why Auntie May kept all those things and all those diaries. But I have an idea, for what it's worth. I think it all started with the death of her father. Ten must be a terrible age for a girl to lose her dad. Then there was the poverty, the constant house moving, the sense of instability – and then the death of her mother, too. I think she clung on to things for the sense of security that they gave her. I am sure she clung on to Denis's things because it was the nearest she could do to clinging on to Denis. I think it was a way of coping with mortality. I think she wrote down every detail of her life so that she could hang on to time itself, and not let it slip through her fingers. She wasn't frightened of death, but she found living with loss almost unbearable.

I think she was odd, unusual, eccentric, yes . . . but I think that she was oddly, unusually and eccentrically virtuous. These days, we think little of old-fashioned virtues like thrift and fortitude, but Auntie May embraced them absolutely. She didn't keep accounts of everything she ever spent and received because she was tight-fisted, but because she was thrifty. She was determined to live within her means so that she wouldn't be a burden to others. Her thriftiness allowed her to be generous – her accounts record countless payments made to any number of charities.

As for fortitude, I can't think of anyone else who would put up with the discomforts that she tolerated without complaint and as a matter of course. The years on a cramped boat, getting up several times a night to pump it out to keep it afloat; the months in the shell of 1 Monkey Row and 36 Baldock Street, with the roof off and rain running down the walls of the sitting room; the years in the Blue Lady caravan, in which the temperatures that she recorded got down as far as 20°F; the many more years in the house that she never got as far as making weatherproof, that got even colder than the caravan and was infested with rats; Auntie May put up with all this, alone and in poor health.

•

During her 1966 holiday Auntie May visited several estate agents and travelled the Devon coastline, looking at building plots. She also did some running repairs on her damaged luggage:

> *FRI. 2.9.66:*
>
> *Fishing tackle etc. shop – Father also does leather repairs like stitching handles onto cases –*
>
> *2 – 6 ft. webbing straps @ 4/-*
> *1 handle (to use with them) 1/9d* } *9.9d*
> *(for small cabin trunk, which is shaky.)*
>
> *Kingsbridge Gazette*   *3d*

She kept and filed the *Kingsbridge Gazette*, of course – I have it on my desk right now. And the trunk, the straps and the carrying handle she bought that day are even now upstairs in the attic of Ware Hall-House.

The following year, Auntie May headed further west, taking a holiday in a caravan in Cornwall. She visited several estate agents, and from the correspondence that she kept, it would seem that one of them, a Mr Braun, of Barnes, Cooke & Company of Hale, managed to interest her in the idea of buying a property rather than moving her house. He must have been a good salesman, because he persuaded her to view several cottages. He even wrote to her on her return to advise her against attempting a rebuild, but when she got back home, there was another letter waiting for her on the mat. It came from the Wells estate agents Andrews & Dewing. It contained the firm's September 1967 Property List. Auntie May immediately underlined one of the entries under 'Building Land' in red ink:

WELLS-NEXT-THE-SEA: Plummers Hill. Outline permission for one dwelling. £500.

She telephoned the agents, who were so confident that the site would suit her that they said they'd give her first refusal. She travelled up to Norfolk on Wednesday, 4 October, and was taken to see the plot. She liked it. She wrote a full description of it in her diary, noting that it was 'Quite secluded from onlookers', and that it was in 'a nice part of town, though no view of sea – near shops, though'. She went and sat on a bench down by the harbour and had a think. Then she went to the council offices in Mill Road, and got the planning permission forms from Mr Rogers. By the time she got home at 10.15 that night, she had filled most of them in.

On Tuesday, 28 November, Auntie May had two surprises. The first was the arrival of a freelance photographer sent by a Norfolk newspaper. She told him she didn't want any press attention as nothing had yet been settled, but he said that the paper would publish the story with or without the pictures, so she let him take some. Then, a telegram arrived, asking her to telephone a Fakenham number reversing the charges. It was from a Mr Fletcher from the Wells Urban District Council. He told her that the local planning committee had approved her application, though the case had to be passed by the county council, too. There had been three reporters present at the meeting, and news of her plans was out. The story appeared in the *Daily Mirror* on Friday, 1 December, and the next day, she found another telegram in her letterbox. This one was from the BBC *Today* programme, asking if she was available to record an interview on Sunday. She sent back a telegram saying she wasn't, and followed it up with a letter explaining that things were still up in the air. 'When matters have sorted themselves out,' she wrote, 'perhaps this will make a better story for you.'

But media interest in Auntie May's story was growing. She came back home on Thursday, 7 December to find 'two young men from the *Daily Telegraph* in the front garden, one of them with a camera'. Pieces and pictures also appeared in the *Times*, the *Eastern Daily Press* and the *London Evening News*. An *Evening Standard* reporter called, followed by photographers from different picture agencies. In the letter she had sent to the BBC on 4 December, she had written 'the whole matter is still in a very tentative state; you see, I do not know yet whether I shall have to move . . .' But the story of a little old lady defying a demolition order by moving her house and rebuilding it with her own hands was unstoppable – even if Auntie May was not quite as old as the published pictures made her look.

At the beginning of February 1967, Auntie May asked for access to next door, as she would need to make drawings of its interior if the building really was to be dismantled. On Friday, 8 February she was given the keys and took Candy into number 36 to see what state it was in. It was pretty derelict. 'The living room floor crumbles as it is walked on,' she wrote. 'The bakehouse floor has collapsed into cellar.' But there were more beams exposed than in her half of the building – and they were big, and in good condition.

From left to right, the Savidge family: Nelly [Cornelia], Henrietta, Frederick and May. Their father died soon after this picture was taken, when May was only 9 years old.

May's Dutch great-grandfather built this lighthouse on the dangerous island coastline of Texel, to stop wreckers from luring ships onto the sands and living off the spoils.

May's fiancé Denis Watson; a Shakespearian actor in London theatres and silent films, he was almost 30 years her senior. Sadly, like May's mother and father, he was to die prematurely.

Picture section designed by David Fletcher Walch

May bought her first home, the Thames river bus *Formosa*, and lived on the river Lee for a number of years, by the Saracen's Head pub, famous for its 'Great Bed of Ware'.

Separated from the rubble of the previous demolitions by a paling fence, May's house in Ware, Hertfordshire awaits destruction, while she desperately negotiates the buying of the bakery next door.

May is rescued from one of her boats (in the background) at Westcliff-on-Sea, Essex; yet another adventure which made headline news in the national press. Sadly the boat sank in the storm that night.

Part of May's medieval house ready for transportation to the seaside a hundred miles away. There were eleven lorry loads and the rebuild would take her the rest of her life.

May in her old caravan where she lived for nearly twenty years during the rebuild. The 'bag lady' look hides her clear-thinking intellect and dogged determination.

All beams were labelled - here is part of the scullery framework. She treated these beams like wayward children that 'moved in the wind' and must be roped and pegged into their correct place.

May had no one to encourage her through the long days, so she used an alarm clock to set herself targets each day. Her diary notes how many nails she extracted each hour.

Thousands of hand-made Hertfordshire peg tiles, awaiting the rebuild. May even made an instrument for forming the oak pegs to hold those tiles onto the roof.

Treating timber against woodworm and rot, May works by the old bakery door which once stood in busy Baldock Street in Ware. It's now a quiet pathway in the back garden, in Norfolk.

A proud photograph developed by May. Luckily, when the 1987 hurricane hit, only a few beams were dislodged. We feared the worst but May didn't even know it had occurred!

Perfecting an oak peg to secure a main beam. May made the old bakery her workshop as the large shop window offered maximum daylight. It was years before she had electricity on site.

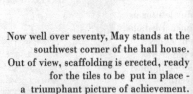

Now well over seventy, May stands at the southwest corner of the hall house. Out of view, scaffolding is erected, ready for the tiles to be put in place - a triumphant picture of achievement.

What a strange concoction of possessions May left for us to find, from childhood bus tickets and piano accordions, to nine side-saddles in the overgrown garden! Every letter was written in duplicate, every sweet paper was filed on the day she ate it: vellum scrolls hidden in toilet roll middles. It was both wonderful and horrific.

Our first task was to make May's scullery habitable - the only room with four good walls. We emptied, cleaned and plastered. How sad that she refused to let us help while she was alive.

May's nephew, Tony, looks out of the window while I chat to his cousin, Sandra. The minstrel's gallery is now under construction, tied up with string, in true Auntie May fashion.

The first completed bedroom. May's father, who was keen on cricket, made the miniature bat for her when she was six years old.

The Great Hall viewed from the cross passage near the front door.

I stand in the completed Great Hall with May's plans in my hand. At last the task is finished and I can live my own life again.

It was at this stage in the story that I first visited Auntie May in Monkey Row. I have already described my own memory of the event and Auntie May records hers in an entry in diary number 146:

SUN: 30.4.67 . . . About 3pm? Chris & Tony arrived – first visit for Chris. TONY photographed the flowering cherry (in colour) – fully out today – and no wind – sun came out for second shot. Tea – (cakes & biscuits) – then they showed the best of their 450 coloured slides of their honeymoon. Marvellous – screen is made of cloth faced with tiny 'pastinilla-like' spheres – sort of luminous. Finished about 8.15pm? Supper – coffee, cheese, bread & butter, watercress, cake. They left about 9.30pm? (first time I've used the rose tea set.) Out late with Candy. (Lent Tony book for Nellie to read, Father Potter of Peckham.) Tony has left an adaptor behind – 2 pin 5 amp socket to bayonet. The lights blew and he replaced the fuses and fixed a wire that had slipped out.

I find Auntie May's account of the visit fascinating. It brings my own memories instantly to life. In my mind's eye, I can see Tony photographing that tree as clearly as if he were doing it right now. It was so close to the house that you could hardly get through the front door. There were roses round the door but they had sagged and you had to duck to get past them. Yes, the sun did come out for a second shot, though if Auntie May hadn't written that down, I don't suppose I would ever have remembered: I suppose it reflects her own interest in photography. I certainly didn't consciously store a memory of what she gave us to eat for tea or supper, but seeing her record of it sets off a little film show in my head: there we all are, holding those pretty teacups . . . the roses on them are pink and Auntie May's has a little chip on the edge of the saucer. It

117

makes me smile to think that she was more interested in describing the screen we projected the pictures on to than the pictures themselves – we were so proud of our adventures and our slides of them! And I can certainly remember the lights blowing.

I had, however, forgotten that she had given Tony a book to pass on to his mother. At the time it seemed to have no significance. Now, though, I think that it is very significant indeed. *Father Potter of Peckham* is the story of an Anglican priest who founded a community called the Brotherhood of the Holy Cross. It describes Father Potter's work in a slum parish, looking after boys and girls at the bottom of the heap. I still have the book, of course – Nellie must have returned it. It is listed in the catalogue of all her books that Auntie May drew up in 1969. The blurb on the cover describes the brotherhood's aim: 'to present the living, loving Christ to the people in a practical way – to poor people, because we love them'. Now that I have read Auntie May's diaries, I can see why she would have liked the book and wanted to share it with her sister. She was deeply, though modestly, religious. She regularly read the Bible – she took it with her on all her trips and holidays. She worshipped every Sunday morning at the chapel of Western House, the geriatric home that had once been the Ware poor house.* Her voluntary work for the Ware Old People's Welfare Association was a practical expression of her faith. There are frequent references in her diaries to visiting the needy: one of those whose names occur most frequently, a Mrs Peck, Auntie May seems to visit almost daily. I can't imagine Auntie May saying anything about presenting the love of Christ to the old and poor people of Ware. But that's what she did.

---

* She was often called upon to play the organ, but it seems she didn't play particularly well. (*SUN 4.8.68 . . . 'played hymns 165, 180 & 370 – but still not fast enough, so I had to miss about half the left hand.'*)

CHAPTER ELEVEN

Embracing the Inevitable

In which Auntie May prepares to move to Norfolk

When Wells Urban District Council approved Auntie May's application for planning permission, Auntie May suddenly became famous. In Hertfordshire, the *Mercury* ran the story on the front page; in Norfolk, the *Eastern Daily Press* and the *Dereham & Fakenham Times* published a photograph of her holding her pet cat, Dinkie, in front of her home at Monkey Row. Nationally, there were pieces and pictures in the *Daily Express*, the *Daily Mirror*, the *London Evening News*, the *Times* and the *Daily Telegraph*. On 8 December 1967, the *Daily Mirror* reported the facts in its own, excited style:

> **Miss May will move home . . . a bit at a time**
>
> FIFTY-SIX-YEAR-OLD spinster May Savidge is moving house – every 500-year-old oak beam and inglenook of it.
>
> She says she is going to knock down her pre-Tudor home and move it to a new site 100 miles away – ALL BY HERSELF.
>
> Then she is going to rebuild it – again all by herself.

Road

For otherwise her local council was to have demolished it to make way for a new relief road.

'It would be heart-breaking to see such a fine old building pulled down,' frail, grey-haired Miss Savidge said yesterday at the house in Ware, Herts.

'I don't see why it's such an impossible idea. I've got nothing to do all day, so I might as well do the job myself.'

Miss Savidge, who is a retired draughtswoman, plans to rebuild the house at Wells in Norfolk.

But there is one snag. The house is semi-detached, so she will have to buy the rest of the building, which has been vacant for three years.

The press reports all described the move as a certainty, but even at this late stage, Auntie May still hoped she would be allowed to stay. Not until the summer of 1968 – six months after her story had hit the press, and fifteen years after she had first heard of the council's plans to demolish her house – did she finally accept the inevitable. On Saturday, 8 June, when the estate agents phoned her to tell her another buyer was interested in the Plummers Hill plot, she made a formal offer of the asking price. The following Monday, she visited the office of her solicitors, Chalmers-Hunt & Bailey of Ware, and instructed them to represent her in the purchase. 'People had said don't buy it until all the drawings had passed,' she wrote, 'but I didn't want to lose it, so I said I would definitely have it, and trust to being able to agree the drawings with the authorities. Don't want to start a hunt for a site all over again.' On Thursday, 27 June 1968, she signed the contract. The die was cast.

Suddenly, the authorities began falling over themselves to help.

I guess that, until then, they must have wondered whether Auntie May would follow through with her plan when it came to it. In mid-September, a Mr Senior from the County Land Agent's department came to tell her that the Hertfordshire County Council would pay her the value of her part of the house as well as allowing her to keep it, provided she dismantled the whole building, took it away, and left the site clear. A month later, he called again, this time to offer some practical advice of his own. He told her that demolition work had started at the nearby pub, the Hope, and suggested she ask the workmen for a batch of tiles that she'd need for her own rebuild. She thanked him, bought £3 worth, and gave the men who delivered them an extra 5s as a tip.

You'd think that once Auntie May's project was under way at last, her diary entries for the summer of 1968 would have been dominated by it – but they are not. She is preoccupied with the problem of Mrs Peck. She isn't going to be around to look after her for much longer, and Mrs Peck is growing increasingly frail and needy. Being housebound, she couldn't collect her pension, so she has given her pension book to her daughter-in-law so that she can collect the money, use it to buy her weekly shopping, and give her the balance. She is also supposed to collect and deliver the heart tablets that Mrs Peck has to take daily. But she often can't manage it. So it falls to Auntie May to buy Mrs Peck's groceries and collect her weekly copy of the *Radio Times*, as well as to make sure she has the right change for the gas meter, to sort out her hearing aid, to get new batteries for her radio and to wind up her clocks – in addition to tending to her increasing nursing needs.

Another thing Mrs Peck couldn't do for herself was tend her children's grave. On Sunday, 21 July 1968, she asked Auntie May to put some flowers on it. She told May that one of the children had died in infancy, and the other, when he was older. Auntie May didn't think it right to ask for any more details, but when she visited the cemetery, she bumped into Mr Powell, the undertaker, who told her that the older Peck child – 'a dear little curly-haired chap, plump' – had drowned in the river. 'He said Mrs P. has never been the same since.'

But Auntie May couldn't spend all her time looking after Mrs Peck. She had a house to move. On Monday, 18 November she went up to Norfolk to take possession of the Plummers Hill plot. She stayed in a guesthouse for a fortnight, during which time she met her new neighbours, Mr and Mrs Hunn, and bought a second-hand caravan from a Mr Smith, 'a bait digger', which she arranged to have towed to the site. She returned on Saturday, 30 November, bringing two presents: a Norfolk tea towel and a stick of Wells rock. Both were for Mrs Peck.

Tony and I, meanwhile, had been rebuilding our own historic home – though we hadn't had to move it from where it had first been built, in Litlington, Cambridgeshire. The experience was later to prove invaluable, though we didn't know that at the time. We had been able to buy the place for a song because it had been due for demolition. It was not much more than a shell of a house, really, and Tony and I were spending all our spare time and energy on restoring and extending it. We were putting down roots. We loved that little cottage. It was called The Nook, and that's just what it was – a little corner of England into which we could retreat; a place of safety, our place. Every barrow-load of concrete, every bucket of plaster, every floorboard and door that we put into it, made it home. I was looking forward to bringing up children in it, launching them into the world from it and eventually, enjoying our retirement in it.

Busy as we were, we kept in touch with Auntie May. We visited her a couple of times a year and exchanged letters, birthday and

Christmas cards, and gifts. When our first child, Polly, was born in January 1969, Auntie May made her a beautifully embroidered pram cover and sent it with a hand-drawn copy of the family tree, tracing Polly's ancestry back to Johannes Kikkert.

Auntie May's diaries describe a quiet Christmas, followed by a period in which she spent a lot of time sorting out Mrs Peck's ear drops and heart pills. Then, in February, she made another trip to Wells to meet builders and planners, and to prepare the site. This time, she stayed in the caravan. It wasn't a very comfortable fortnight. When she arrived on 6 February, the weather was bitterly cold and the caravan door wouldn't close properly. She had to tie it shut with string. When she went to light the stove, she noticed that there was no glass in its door, so there was no way of controlling the draught. The fire burned far too fast, then went out. When it got dark, she turned on the gas to light the lamp, but found that the pipe leaked, so she had to turn it off again and manage with a candle. She lay down under the three blankets she had brought, but couldn't get warm. When she woke up the next morning, she found that the fumes had given her a blinding headache and the thermometer in the caravan was showing 32°F – freezing point. The next night was even worse. 'Awful night,' she wrote. 'Heavy snow, strong N. wind . . . caravan rocked a bit, & leans to the S., anyway. Fire would not light – too late to try any more – no gas – had a candle and the Beatrice stove in the evening.' When she woke up in the morning, the thermometer had dropped to 22°F.

But there were positive things to record, too. Her new neighbours, the Hunns, were friendly and helpful. They allowed her free access to their water, made her cups of tea, gave her a pint of milk and kindling for her stove, and when Mr Hunn went sea fishing, he brought back a fine cod as a present. She gave the head to the cat. Her meetings with Mr Terrington, who was to build the foundations, were all encouraging. She sorted out access to the sewers with Mr Rogers from the planning department. The Norfolk end of the project was starting to come together.

After a week back in Ware, she returned to Wells for a few days to get some important jobs done. She got the caravan levelled and stabilised, and mended the door. She made a start on putting up the garden fence. She drew a nameplate on a postcard and fixed it to the gate in the wall: 'Ware Hall-House Site'. She also met several other near neighbours, who invited her in for cups of tea. Mrs Hunn took her as a guest to a Women's Institute meeting, at which the speaker presented a slide show about Norfolk. Auntie May was beginning to feel at home.

What she hadn't yet done, though, was decide how she was going to get the house from Ware to Wells. One option she was considering was moving the frame by road – in one piece. The idea came in a letter from an admiring stranger in California:

King City, California, U.S.A.
January 8, 1968

Dear Miss Savidge:

In a Stockton, California, newspaper there appeared last month a short but interesting article about you and your 500-year-old home which the local council has marked down for demolishing to make way for a new road.

The article went on to say that in order to keep your home you are planning to knock it down piece by piece and rebuild it on a new plot of land 100 miles away as a 'do it yourself' exercise.

This interested me so much that I felt I wanted to take the liberty of writing to you to tell you how I admire your courage and 'spunk', as well as the ambition to undertake such an enormous job. I would be so interested in learning of your progress and final success. I have the highest praise for anyone wishing to preserve old buildings. Here in the western part of the United States, buildings only 50 years old are constantly being demolished to be replaced by more modern structures. However, many small homes, if they are of frame construction, that is wooden, are sold and moved to another location to make room for new freeways. I'm enclosing an amusing clipping of such a moving project recently nearby.

I am a widow of 68 and live in the frame house my father built over 80 years ago. He moved it at one time from one end of this 160 acre farm to the other end, but sawed it in two and moved each half separately on large rollers. I was born in this house, as no doubt you were in yours, and I understand only too well how you must love your home.

I wish you the best of luck in your re-building project. If ever you have time to spare to write to me how you are progressing with it, I would be most happy to hear from you.

Sincerely,

Mrs. Fred Koester.

The 'amusing clipping'* Mrs Koester enclosed described a journey on wheels made by a three-bedroom, 26ft-wide house up a narrow canyon: 'The first mile was uneventful except for swerving tracks cut by the heavy equipment. Beyond that point the road still looked this morning as if it had been visited by a capricious tornado.'

But Auntie May took the idea seriously, as I discovered when I was going through her correspondence files for the following year:

---

* The article is not dated and the newspaper is not named.

PICKFORDS LIMITED
HEAD OFFICE
HEAVY HAULAGE SERVICE
52 BEDFORD ROW
LONDON, W.C. 1

01-405-4399

Miss M. Savidge,
1, Monkey Row, Ware,
Herts.
28th March 1969

Dear Miss Savidge,

Thank you for your letter of the 26th March, from which I note that you hope to be able to move your cottage from Ware to a site in Norfolk.

Whilst it is true that we move a number of unusual loads I must say that we have no experience in the movement of cottages.

I cannot tell from your letter whether your hope is that the cottage should be moved fully erected or whether you wish it to be dismantled and erected on the site. If you are looking for a firm to carry out the dismantling and re-erection then I am afraid we cannot assist you.

However, if a fully erected move is envisaged then I would be happy to discuss the problems with you at my office at 11.0 a.m. on Wednesday the 26th March. In order that the matter can be discussed it will be necessary for you to provide the dimensions, i.e. length, breadth and height.

I must say that I feel that it is highly improbable that a fully erected move will be possible due to the age of the cottage and the restrictions on the route in the form of overhead bridges and narrow roads.

However, I will be available on 26th March if you wish to see me at the address shown at the head of this letter.

Yours sincerely

E.G. Milne

Asst. Chief Heavy Haulage Manager.

Auntie May did meet the man from Pickfords, and it was immediately clear that moving the house in one piece by road was a non-starter. But then she had another idea:

> 1, *Monkey Row,*
> *Ware,*
> *Herts.*
> 5th May, 1969

The Officer in Charge,
Coltishall Helicopter Airfield
Near Norwich
Norfolk.

Dear Sir,

For several years Herts. County Council has been planning to build a new road in Ware, and it will come right through my little house. This is a very interesting timber-framed building, about 500 years old, having a central hall with rooms above it, and originally, a fire in the middle of the floor, the smoke finding its own way out. Later, a Tudor chimney stack was inserted, also two more bedrooms, and the building divided into two little residences. The building is on the list of Ancient Monuments and Historic Buildings, but this does not seem to count when a road is proposed, so I wrote to Herts. County Council in 1963, stating that I wished to re-erect the house if it was in the way of the road.

Since then, I have bought a piece of land in Wells-next-the-Sea, and obtained permission from the U.D.C. and Norfolk County Council to use it for this purpose. So many old houses have been destroyed already, and I feel that we have no right to keep destroying the things of the past.

It was my intention to take the timber frames to pieces and put them together again on the site. The joints are fixed with tapered wooden pegs, which can be very difficult to get out. Six months ago, I was informed that I had until April, 1970, at the earliest, to do the job, but now suddenly I hear that the round-about may be built first, and that I may have to clear the site by the end of August, 1969, — an extremely difficult job.

Therefore I am wondering if it would be possible to lift the framework by helicopter, to save the time in taking it to pieces. It is oak, and I worked out the weight to about eight tons. Am told that British helicopters will only carry about four to five tons, and if this is so, I wonder if you would be so kind as to let me know whether there is a U.S.A. helicopter that could tackle it please? — and if so, who I should write to. The roof timbers weigh about three tons, and could be separated from the rest of the structure if necessary, which would then be reduced to about five tons, but it would be much quicker to have the framework moved complete, and lowered on to the new foundations.

I would, of course, wish to pay towards the expenses, but hope they would not be too heavy, as I am not a wealthy person.

Anything which you can suggest towards getting this framework moved from Ware to Wells-next-the-Sea, will be greatly appreciated. Most Hall-houses are very much larger, and were either Manor houses or farm houses, where the employees lived in; this is one of the smallest to have been found, and I do want to save it for future generations.

Hoping very much that you can help in some way,
Yours truly,
May Savidge
Encl. S.A.E. 5ᵈ

•

202 Squadron Detachment Royal Air Force
Coltishall
Norwich
Norfolk
NOR 64Y

Coltishall 361 Ext 491

13th May 1969

COLT/202D/6/2/Air
Miss M. Savidge
1, Monkey Row
Ware
Herts

Dear Miss Savidge

Thank you for your letter of 5th May 1969 relating to the prospect of providing an air lift for the framework of your house at Ware.

As the officer responsible for the Rescue Helicopter Unit at Coltishall, the Station Commander has instructed me to investigate the problem and write to you direct.

We, of course, act under the orders of the Ministry of Defence, and I regret that it is highly unlikely that the use of service helicopters would be authorised for this purpose. There is however, a further consideration. *The heaviest vertical lifting capacity within the Royal Air Force was achieved with the Belvedere Helicopter. These machines, based in the Far East could lift a maximum of six thousand pounds (under three tons). Unfortunately, the Belvedere has recently been withdrawn from service. Other machines currently in use in this country have a capacity of under two tons and at this weight their cross-country range is severely limited.*

With these unhelpful facts in mind I made contact with the Senior Pilot of Bristow's Helicopters Ltd at Gt Yarmouth to see what non-military lifting capacity is available in this country. It seems that apart from the big amphibious S61 Helicopter (which has no underslinging facility), there would appear to be no machine in current use that could take on such a large task.

Concerning the very last resort in your suggestion of the USAF based in this country, I have no specific information, but I am almost certain their machines are the smaller types, such as our own, established for Search and Rescue purposes.

I trust these details answer your questions on the matter and though unable to offer any physical assistance, I wish you well with this most interesting project.

Sincerely,

(R. J. LAWRENCE)
Flight Lieutenant
Officer Commanding

•

May decided to check with the Americans anyway and wrote on 25 May to the US Embassy in Grosvenor Square, enclosing a 5d stamp to cover the cost of their reply, and asking if they might be able to help.

EMBASSY OF THE UNITED STATES OF AMERICA
OFFICE OF THE AIR ATTACHE

24 Grosvenor Square London, W.1

Miss Mary [sic] Savidge
1, Monkey Row
Ware, Herts.

Reference is made to your letter of 25 May 1969 requesting assistance for the re-erection of Ware Hall-House at Wells-next-the-Sea, Norfolk.

While the United States Military Services have often helped people in their host country as a good-neighbor policy, we are, unfortunately, unable to help you with your request. Neither the United States Air Force nor the United States Army has helicopters available in Britain which could perform the task you desire.

You may wish, however, to contact a local contractor who would know where helicopters of the size and lifting power required to move your house are available.

Sincerely,

JAMES V. REGAN

Major, USAF Assistant Air Attache

So, that was that. The idea of flying the house to Wells was a nonstarter.

Meanwhile, Auntie May's diaries show that she was still worrying about who would look after Mrs Peck. She brought the subject up at a meeting of the executive committee of the Ware Old People's Welfare Association on 10 April. The committee undertook to make sure that care for Mrs Peck would continue.

Mrs Peck was worrying, too. On 13 April, Auntie May got a lift up to Norfolk, where she spent another fortnight.

13.4.69: Called on <u>Mrs. Peck</u> (didn't have time, before.) She cried —
I wish someone else would visit her in my place before I really have to
go. Gave her Radio Times and swapped 6/- for gas. *She came to the*
door suddenly and put her arms round me and kissed me — poor old
soul — I'm not going for long.

Auntie May spent the following two weeks preparing the site for
the arrival of lorries, and planning the foundations and drains with
Mr Terrington.

MON 14.4.69: . . . <u>Mrs. Terrington</u> is quite sure I will never re-erect
the house — her grandfather was a builder and she has spent her life
connected with it all. It was difficult to finish a sentence to Mr.
Terrington or to both — he was looking at the drawing — she said I
wouldn't get any help as everyone was busy (builders, that is) — I only
wanted an estimate for the foundations and drains — Mr. T. said they
would take about a month from date of starting — Mrs. T. asked if I
had ever re-erected a house before — also what figures I had — I said
no-one had quoted any figures — . . . she thought would take 10 months
— with men, I think — don't know how many.

When Auntie May got back to Ware, she found a letter from the
county council requiring her to clear the Monkey Row site by the
end of August. Things were hotting up. Meanwhile, Mrs Peck was
getting increasingly ill and confused:

MON 2.6.69: Out again just before 6.45 to Mrs. Peck — she was
awake, still looking very groggy — pain in L. side when she breathes,
pain in region of waist line (front) — pain in middle of chest. Still

---

* That is, she gave Mrs Peck the right coins for her gas meter.

vomiting – including a lot of phlegm! She had a bit of jelly, which seemed to have stayed down, but doesn't want food. She is still climbing up to close heavy curtain, in case she gets into trouble for showing a light – she <u>still</u> doesn't realise that that's only a wartime offence. She knows that the street lights are on. Said I'd let the Dr. know – she kept saying 'I don't want to go away'.

Auntie May visited her daily. She fetched her small bottles of stout, essence of peppermint and home-made jellies. She sorted out her lamps and clocks, filled her hot-water bottle, made up her bed, emptied her chamber pot, made sure she took her pills, and rubbed her back with camphorated oil to ease the pain. Another Old People's Welfare worker, Mrs Brogden, was also visiting and bringing food, but Mrs Peck ate and drank little. Auntie May got the Salvation Army to call, too, and Mrs Peck's daughter-in-law made more frequent appearances. The doctor called several times:

MON 16.6.69: Dr. confirmed nothing organically wrong – he said he had thought there was, but the C. Hospital had said not. He thinks it must be <u>wind</u> & <u>worry</u>.

The following Friday evening, when Auntie May called on Mrs Peck, she found the door fastened, which was not usual, and she could see through the window that the bed was empty and the covers had been thrown back. She knelt on the window ledge so that she could see if Mrs Peck had fallen onto the floor, but she hadn't. She called on Mrs Cakebread next door, who told her that Mrs Peck's daughter-in-law had visited that morning and had been so alarmed by the state of her that she had called the doctor, who had suspected an internal haemorrhage and sent for an ambulance. Mrs Peck had been taken to Bishop's Stortford Hospital. The following morning, Mrs Brogden called at Monkey Row to ask Auntie May if she wanted to accompany her to the hospital. 'I would have been glad,' writes Auntie May, 'but really must get on with moving job – 3 weeks delay, now, over Mrs P.'s illness'.

Just how much had to be done is reflected in the length of entries in Auntie May's diaries. At this point, they get longer and longer. There are lots of St John Ambulance loose ends to tie up, and the letters from Pickfords, the RAF and the American Embassy have convinced her that the only way to move the house is to take it apart first. She spends a great deal of time trying to hunt down a builder with suitable lorries for the job, and makes arrangements to spend some more time in Norfolk to make sure that the foundations and drainage arrangements are precisely right before the dismantled house arrives. She keeps daily tabs on Mrs Peck by telephoning the hospital and Mrs Brogden. She learns that she is going to be in hospital for at least six weeks.

In Norfolk, Auntie May was shocked to find how overgrown the garden had become since she had last seen it. (I know just how she must have felt!) The grass was seeding, and there were brambles and nettles everywhere. She had to clear it all so that the precise position of the foundation slab could be pegged out. On most days, she was up before 4.30am so that she could work before it got too hot. She returned on 2 July. The following morning, she learned that Mrs Peck had died the previous day.

On Saturday, 5 July Auntie May went to see the undertaker, Mr Powell, to ask about the funeral. 'He spoke about her life – she was about eighteen when they took her little son home in his coffin, & he's never forgotten her distress, in all these years of funerals.' The service was held the following Tuesday at the Salvation Army hall in Ware. Auntie May brought a 'spray of yellow and red flowers (roses, carnations, chrysanthemums and laurels)'. A week later, she met the health visitor, who told her the cause of Mrs Peck's death. She had been suffering from cancer of the stomach.

Having discharged her final duty to Mrs Peck, Auntie May threw herself into the urgent task of stripping out both halves of the house. She got hold of an old oil drum, chained it to a post in the garden, and started a bonfire in it that was to burn more or less constantly for the next eleven months. She knocked through into number 36 and found it in a very poor state, though she was impressed by the size of the ancient beams that had never been covered up. It was hard and dangerous work:

> *TUE: 15.7.69: . . . Into 36 again . . . Fixed rope around counter, and myself, and went down into cellar — brought some more rotten wood up and put some on incinerator — not much — burning very slowly . . .*

In the autumn of that year, Auntie May was back in the papers again. She had cut a deal with the local authority in which she was to be given the other half of the house in return for demolishing the whole building and taking it away. The *Daily Telegraph* of Saturday, 20 September reported that: 'Every brick, beam and timber of the house will be numbered by Miss Savidge, who will reconstruct it like a giant jigsaw puzzle. "It will take a long time to complete and I will live in a caravan while I am working on the site. I just won't have such a marvellous old house bulldozed into the ground," she said.'

Tony and I offered to help, but Auntie May wasn't having any of it. She was determined to do as much work as possible herself. She prepared for the move meticulously. First, she made a set of detailed drawings of the house. This was a particularly challenging task, as the shape of it had been dictated by the irregular hand-hewn timbers used to make its framework. There were no right angles in the building and the parallel walls were not quite of equal length. She joked that she had been well prepared for this by her wartime work in the drawing office of De Havilland, for there were no right angles in a Mosquito, either! Then she painted a number on each individual timber – so that it could be identified when the time came to reassemble the framework – and marked the numbers on her plans. Press reports that she numbered the bricks, too, were an exaggeration. Auntie May knew that the brick infilling had been done long after the house had originally been built, and the order in which they were put back didn't matter. However, on one visit, I did find her using greaseproof paper and a crayon to make a rubbing of the brickwork in one of the fireplaces. I wondered whether she was losing her marbles, but she had a perfectly logical explanation. 'I have never laid a brick in my life,' she said. 'I am not quite sure which bond this is. It might be Flemish, or perhaps Old English. I have got to reproduce it and I want to get it right. Besides, I need to know how thick to lay the mortar, because if it is too thin, I am going to have to buy more Elizabethan bricks, and I can't afford that on my pension.'

The demolition was just as painstakingly methodical. First, she had the house surrounded by scaffolding, and then she supervised a team of local demolition contractors as they took the place carefully apart, tile by tile, beam by beam, and brick by brick. To prevent anyone stealing anything from the site, she continued to live in the house while they worked, only moving into the workshop at the bottom of the garden when the outside walls were finally taken down. Then she oversaw the loading of the parts of the house on to a Bedford lorry, which made the 200-mile round trip to Norfolk eleven times.

But it was obvious that she would never be able to get the site cleared by the original deadline and, on 25 August, the authorities sent her a letter extending it to 31 December. Auntie May received it with relief, but she could see that even that leeway was scarcely enough. Still – at least she now had a firm idea of how she would move the building. A piece of paper I found in her filing cabinet describes the plan in detail:

CONTRACT

I, William Robert Smith, of 1, Cundalls Road, Proprietor of Ware Demolition Co., undertake, for the sum of Three hundred pounds (£300), to demolish carefully the oak-framed house known as 36, Baldock Street and 1, Monkey Row, measuring 47′6″ by about 18′6″, but excluding the more modern extension used as a kitchen and W.C., and also excluding the workshop known as 9, Monkey Row. The materials and fittings are for re-use by the owner, May Alice Savidge, for the re-erection of the whole house in Norfolk. The bricks will be cleaned and the half-bricks saved, also the half tiles. If the re-use of the mortar, hair plaster, and mud and chaff is advised,* these will be kept separate from each other and bagged up. The owner will number the timbers as they are uncovered, and draw them on the plan and elevations. Unwanted rubble, etc., will be put in the cellar, to help fill it in, as Herts. County Council requires the site to be left tidy, and to be cleared by 31st December, 1969, at the latest. Public Liability Insurance has been taken out by the owner, but not Insurance for any personal injury, and no claim will be made on her should an accident occur.

W.R. Smith, WARE DEM. Co.
M. Savidge
Witnessed by
L.W. Gilling

---

* It wasn't. Auntie May wrote to the Society for the Protection of Ancient Buildings, and they advised against it.

What that contract doesn't mention is that Auntie May would continue to live in the house while they took it down. The conditions she put up with were unimaginable, as Tony and I saw when we visited later that year – the last time we saw her in Hertfordshire. Outside, the temperature was freezing, and inside it wasn't any higher, for the demolition men had taken off the roof. She was living in the downstairs sitting room, and there was nothing between her and the sky but the plaster of its ceiling and the floorboards of the room above. There was so little of the building left standing that Auntie May had to sleep in a little office room in the workshop that she called her 'shed'. She was wearing several coats, one over the other, and a woollen hat was tied to her head with a scarf. There was no electricity supply on the site. At night, the only light came from a hurricane lamp and she boiled the water for a pot of tea on a Victorian paraffin stove that she lit with mittened hands. She apologised for having already packed the best china, and poured my tea into a cup that was so badly cracked I had to pour what leaked into the saucer back into the cup as fast as I could drink it. We were horrified at the squalor of it all, but Auntie May just didn't seem to notice.

Tony told her that snow had been forecast and that when it melted, it would bring down her ceiling. She dismissed this as nonsense and said that in any case, it didn't matter – the worst that could happen would be that the plaster would fall down and she was going to have to knock it down soon, anyway. We said our goodbyes, but when we got to the car, we decided that we just couldn't leave her exposed to the elements like that. We went to the nearest builders' merchant and bought a huge sheet of polythene. Then we drove back to what was left of the house, climbed up the scaffolding, and covered the first-floor floorboards with the polythene, weighing it down with bricks. Auntie May politely thanked us for our efforts, but assured us that they really hadn't been necessary. But the next day, it did snow – and heavily. Heaven only knows what would have happened if we hadn't put down that plastic sheet.

In early December, Auntie May received a surprise in the post. It was a letter from the BBC offering her a 'Charlie Chester Award', which would be presented on the radio programme to be aired on New Year's Day. It was a significant accolade: Charlie Chester's weekly *Sunday Soapbox* show on the *Light Programme* drew an audience of millions. May wrote back immediately to accept. She had no interest in personal fame or recognition; she saw it as a chance to draw attention to the wider threat to historic buildings throughout the land.

But there was a problem. She was nervous about leaving the site. To the outside world, it no longer looked like any kind of home – and local youngsters had started to use the surrounding area as a kind of adventure playground. Her diaries recorded numerous close encounters with unsavoury youths. One of her friends, Miss Virgo – 'I don't know how I would manage without her' – came to the rescue. She offered to house-sit while Auntie May took part in the programme.

Before that, though, there was Christmas – the last that Auntie May would spend in what was left of her Hertfordshire home. She celebrated it alone. She could hardly invite anyone to a meal on a demolition site and she couldn't accept an invitation to go elsewhere, because she felt she had to stay and guard the dismantled elements of her house. Her Christmas dinner was not quite the traditional feast:

THURS: CHRISTMAS DAY –1969.
Midnight Service on Radio 4 – till 1.15 a.m.

Dull, damp — drips stopped during day . . .

Opened some things from larder (now gone) —
1966 Luncheon meat (tin)
1959 tomatoes (small tin)
19—? Stewed apples (Kilner jar)
19—? Robertson's mincemeat (1lb jar)
Simmered the last 2 together, with sugar — something like Christmas
pudding! — eaten with bread and marg. — could have mixed the bread
in, too.

On New Year's Eve she 'took coffee etc. to shed office to hear Charlie Chester show'. It must have been a strange way to end the year. I doubt that she recognised the irony of it. All over the nation, people were sitting comfortably before their fires, their families around them, listening to a programme that celebrated her spirit and determination; she was listening to the same programme alone, in a freezing shed on what looked like a bomb site, wondering whether her determination would achieve anything at all. The project was taking far longer than she had estimated. The church bells that marked the ending of the year also marked the passing of the authorities' latest deadline for clearing the site, even if they had made no threats to enforce it.

CHAPTER TWELVE

'This Is Our Home Now!'

In which Auntie May, Candy and Dinkie
move to Wells

A week later, May made a diary entry in capital letters, and underlined it twice:

WEDS: 7.1.70 – LETTER FROM MR TERRINGTON – SITE READY!

On 12 January '2 young men from County Hall came . . . they said they hadn't come to harry me, just to see how I was getting on. I was glad – the date has been worrying me'. In fact, Auntie May was getting on quite well. Mr Smith and his team were now taking apart the main beams of the house, and she was marking those beams with numbers and recording their position on the plan she had drawn of the house. She was also listing the order in which the timbers were taken down in her diary. I can't say it makes interesting reading, but I do find it remarkable that she should have decided to record every act in the process in such extraordinary detail:

FRI: 16.1.70 . . . Scraped muck from top of S.21 (to dry off, for

marking) & from front of B1.J.26 – (very wet). Cleared up the mess.
Quick lunch in shed, then painted numbers on S.21 & E.1 . . .

Despite the rain and the snow, things were going well, and Auntie
May was able to arrange for the first lorry load of building parts to
be moved to Wells at the end of the month.

SAT: 31.1.70 . . . Monk & Hawkins lorry had arrived by 8.20 am. –
3 men and a boy. Loaded up first Tudor bricks and left at mid-day.
Mr S. stays helping demolishing.

The move had begun, and Auntie May was clearly looking forward
to getting to Wells; but she was also looking forward to getting
away from the demolition site:

SUN: 1.2.70 – gang of long haired youths with sacks hanging around
– I shall be glad to get away from here – it was bad enough when it
was a car park, but it is worse now. There should be some privacy from
public & some peace in the Norfolk garden. Candy has barked herself
hoarse again . . .

On Monday, 2 February, Miss Virgo came to stand guard while
Auntie May went off to Wells on one of the lorry trips. Her diary
shows a rare glimpse of excitement. She had a 'lovely windscreen
view' of the sunrise and noticed 'just a sweep of clouds across the
sky' – but she didn't think much of the musical taste of the lorry's
driver: 'deafening Radio One, etc. – don't know how anyone could
drive with such a noise'.

When the lorry reached Norfolk, Auntie May went to see Mr
Terrington and paid him for his work on the foundations. She then
returned to Ware to supervise the loading of the rest of the

building. The lorry made two trips on Wednesday, and on Thursday a reporter and photographer from the *Daily Sketch* turned up. Much of the main structure of the house was now down, but the shell of the kitchen extension of the Monkey Row half was still there and Auntie May was still occupying it. The workshop that housed her stored furniture was still standing, too, and Auntie May was still sleeping in it.

That February, heavy snow was followed by freezing fog and hard frosts. In March, what Auntie May describes as 'the worst snow in the SE in living memory' started to fall:

> *SUN: 8.3.70 . . . Shed office 30 deg F* – *Very sharp frost* – *had left tap dripping into kettle in sink and there was a large icicle between tap and kettle with lots of additions at the lower end: ice outside spout, kettle frozen to sink: sink outlet frozen, but tap still dripping! Sun out about 8 am. Breakfast* – *kitchen* – *milk frozen.*

Outside, the smoke from her incinerator mingled with the smoke from the bonfire that was once the Hope pub, and drifted across a frozen snowscape. But the big move wouldn't be long now. She would soon be in Wells, and starting the next phase of the project – and she was looking forward to it. When she phoned HC Lewis of Fakenham to arrange storage of all her boxes, she wrote 'Norfolk accents sounded quite homely'. On Monday, 16 March, she accompanied the van that took her furniture to Norfolk for storage. Candy and Dinkie came too, so Miss Virgo didn't have to stay. The following day, May's sister Nellie and her husband Bern came to visit, bringing some cakes and a trifle. Their visit coincided with the removal of the last beam of the framework – number S.21 – and they all had a piece of cake to celebrate.

There was still a lot of clearing and sorting to do, of course, and this was made more difficult by several days of rain. The kitchen and WC extension were still standing and, though the wall between the kitchen and the rest of the building was gone, Auntie May got Mr Smith to nail one of the doors over the gap. She also got him to put some old planks down on the floor as duckboards, for the whole site was now covered in slimy mud. The place must have looked like a First World War battlefield but, among all the wreckage, Auntie May managed to turn a corner of her half-demolished kitchen into a darkroom for developing the photographs she was taking of the work. On Tuesday, 20 January another newspaper reporter visited, and a woman whom Auntie May did not know called at the site to say that she had heard the story on the radio and would like to offer her a bed. Auntie May refused – 'I said I had to keep an eye on things here.'

Tony and I had seen Auntie May's living conditions at this time, and had done what little we could to improve them, but when I read her record of them many years later, I felt painfully guilty. If a complete stranger could offer to take her in and look after her, surely we, her family, could have done more? Why hadn't we offered to stand guard over the site for a day or two, so that she could take a break, and be warm and comfortable even if only for a short time? I suppose the answer is that we knew that she would refuse any help – though I still feel bad about it. But I also feel curious. By any imaginable standards, Auntie May's circumstances were intolerable. Why did she put up with them without complaint? Why didn't she make things at least a little easier for herself?

I think the simple answer is that she just didn't notice. She seems to have been utterly single-minded. Having decided on the great task she was to perform, she concentrated on it, seeing any inconveniences encountered along the way as incidental. She didn't dwell upon them any more than she ever dwelt upon herself. Others might see her as a stoic, but she didn't seem to think of herself as enduring anything; she was just getting on with what she had to do, dealing with things as they turned up. It was an attitude that left strangers amazed, and those of us that cared for her wringing our hands in horror. Nellie found it particularly trying: as her elder sister, she felt it was her duty to save May from herself – but she never succeeded and her offers of help or guidance were always rebuffed.

On Monday, 16 March, Auntie May made another day trip to Wells – this time in the cab of the van from Ware Furnishing that she had hired to take her furniture to Fakenham. She took Candy and Dinkie with her, and was pleased to see that Dinkie seemed quite at home, prowling confidently about the garden and caravan. When Auntie May got back at the end of the day, she was too tired to move the things heaped up on her armchair in the shed 'office', so she slept sitting on a box, leaning against the wall.

The weather improved in April and Auntie May took advantage of it. She used her pushchair to move a lot of the boxes of her possessions to Place House, the home of a 'Mr. W.' who had invited her to store her things there so that Mr Smith could knock down the workshop in which she had been keeping them. The end of the project was in sight. One of the last loose ends to tie up was the beautiful, double-flowering cherry tree that had stood outside the front door. Auntie May wanted to dig it up and take it with her, but wasn't sure if it would be possible. On Wednesday, 29 April she went to the nearby telephone box and called the Hertfordshire Training School – '*(Ware 3666)*' – to ask for advice. They told her she needed to ask a tree specialist, but Auntie May's record of the phone call is interesting – not because of what was said, but because of something that happened while she was making it:

2 young policemen opened door of 'phone box & one said 'Are you all
right?' – they'd had a call that I had a handkerchief over the 'phone
– I said I always do use a Dettol hanky over the mouthpiece – have
done for years – said I once got an awful cold, after using a 'phone that
looked as if someone had been breathing heavily onto it. I keep one
special hanky – one policeman smelt it, to check – they also took my
name and address – they said they get a lot of queer calls around this
way – I suppose someone thought I was muffling my voice, but a single
layer of Dettol hanky doesn't do that. I said that at work the 'phones
were cleaned & disinfected regularly – but public ones are very germy
things.

Auntie May was happy to live in the roofless shell of a house in
mid-winter and sleep in a caravan that was ten degrees below
freezing, but she wouldn't pick up a public phone without wrapping
it in a disinfectant-soaked hanky for fear of catching a cold. When
I read that, I couldn't suppress a laugh!

During May, Auntie May made several more trips accom-
panying bricks, beams and tiles on the Monk & Hawkins lorry. She
planned to make the big move on 1 June, but there was one more
problem to be dealt with. The possessions she had stored in the
shed/workshop and its outside toilet were all gone: it was time for
those outbuildings to be pulled down, along with what little was left
of the kitchen. Where would she sleep while that was happening?
Miss Virgo couldn't offer to help – she was in hospital – but when
Auntie May telephoned to ask after her on Thursday, 28 May, Miss
Virgo's companion, Miss Page, invited Auntie May to spend her
last two nights in Hertfordshire at 121 Watton Road, where they
lived with their chickens and goats. Miss Virgo's sister, Dorothy,
was also staying, so that she could be near to the hospital.

Saturday, 30 May was a fine day, but the move didn't get off to a very good start. Soon after the lorry and three men turned up at 7.30am, they all realised that there was too much stuff to go in the last trip planned for the following Monday. By noon, they could fit nothing more on, so they set off to Wells with what they had. There was talk of making another trip the next day, but nothing could be confirmed until they got back to the office.

> *About 4.30 pm. Miss Page & Miss D. Virgo called on way back from hospital, but I was still very busy clearing up and covering up, in case stuff has to stay until next Sat. – with no one to look after it.*
>
> *Miss Page came back for me after milking goats etc. – about 8.30 pm. – we put several things in her car – some coats, etc., clean clothes, bread bin of food, towels, barometer, zither in blue washing bag – etc. – & Candy and Dinkie and myself – and she took me home to 121 W. Rd. Lovely refreshing evening meal (vegetarian) – & grape juice & soda water – also lovely bath – first one since Sept. – slept on camp bed in front room, downstairs, with Candy & Dinkie – such a joy to be where folks treat animals as important. Tried to 'phone Monk & H about 10 pm, as they had not 'phoned – no answer.*

Auntie May phoned them again at 8.30am the following morning, but she needn't have worried, for by the time she got to the site, the men were already there and at work. They were ready to go at noon. Auntie May stayed behind for a final tidy up, turned off the water at the mains stopcock, and picked up the thrift plant that she had dug up and the men had left behind. She carried it back to 121 Watton Road in a washing-up bowl.

She was up at 5.30am the following morning, ready to make her very last trip to the Monkey Row site. Dorothy Virgo made her breakfast; Miss Page refused to accept anything in return for her stay. The two of them helped her carry her things to the lorry. The driver loaded up the last things to go, including a pair of cast-iron bed ends and a tea chest, and Auntie May, Candy and Dinkie joined him in the cab. They got to Wells at 10.30am. Auntie May telephoned Mr Smith, the bait digger, to let him know that she had arrived and was ready for his help – and he and his brother came immediately. By 3.30pm, the job was done. The Smiths left to deliver the bait they had dug earlier that morning. The driver had a wash at the tap, and returned to Hertfordshire. Auntie May gave him a pound note as a tip.

Auntie May did some more clearing up, in case it rained – but it didn't. Then she looked around the garden in which she was to rebuild her house. The apple blossom was over, but the clematis and the lily of the valley and the strawberry plants were in flower. When she picked up the boots she had left in the Blue Lady caravan, a florin dropped out of one of them. She wrote the extra 2s in the accounts column of her diary, bringing the running total to £15 3s 5d. Just above it, she had already written in blue biro: 'Candy & Dinkie & I stayed – this is our home now.' She picked up a red pen, underlined it again, and drew a box round it. The second phase of her project had finally begun. She had celebrated her fifty-ninth birthday at the beginning of the week. She was five days into the sixtieth year of her life.

CHAPTER THIRTEEN

Rebuilding Begins

In which Auntie May makes a slow start and
encounters some unexpected difficulties

Auntie May recorded the big move in diary number 190. Two
hundred and fifty diaries and twenty-three years later, she still
hadn't finished rebuilding the house. The diaries in which she
recorded every detail of the reconstruction are a catalogue of
patiently borne difficulties. Looking back on it now, it is easy to see
why it all took so long. Anybody who has ever built a house from
scratch will know how hard it is to coordinate the stages of the
operation. A large building firm that employs tradesmen directly
can order them to turn up at the appropriate time. A small builder
who sub-contracts work to others has some sort of hold on them –
they know that if they let him down, he won't offer them further
work. Auntie May was her own project manager on a one-off
project, and thus completely at the mercy of all the tradesmen and
labourers she had to employ. Some of them were loyal and reliable;
others were not. I started to count the number of times Auntie May
wrote 'Mr X did not turn up again' or 'Mr Y <u>still</u> hasn't come, as
promised', but I gave up. The diaries are peppered with phrases
like that.

Another thing that slowed everything down was Auntie May's

decision not to employ anyone to do anything she could do herself. She believed that her tough upbringing had prepared her for nearly all the practical challenges she now faced. She said as much in an address to the Fakenham Ladies Circle Club in the spring of 1971. She called her talk *Dismantling & Re-erection of Ware Hall-House*:

Looking through my notes, and trying to collect my thoughts on this move, it really seems as if everything has led up to it. For instance, my mother more or less brought us up on the maxim that 'there is no such word as "can't"', and I think this had a marked effect on my life. Another favourite saying was 'worse troubles at sea' – and she had reason to know what she was talking about.

My father was an engineer, and I was always attracted to engineering, and to practical things like 'what makes the wheels go round'. But although women had worked on munitions during the First World War, engineering was still not considered to be suitable for girls when I was young, and my father had died just before I was ten, so we had rather lost touch with the engineering world.

I started work as assistant to a wallpaper designer, and later became designer to a small silk printing firm. During the slump, I was lucky to get a job in an office, and in the evenings I learnt shorthand and typing, which came in very useful, later.[*] Fairly early in the Hitler War, I had the chance to go back to drawing – either on maps for the Admiralty, or on an engineering draughtsmanship course, which was the one I chose. We did some practical work, as well as drawing, as one should know how to <u>make</u> anything that one <u>draws</u>.[†]

[*] In the margin at this point, Auntie May has written 'Indicate pile of letters'. She certainly had plenty to choose from!

[†] Alas, I have only been able to find the first two pages of her typed draft of this talk. The rest has gone adrift.

May's combination of determination, inexperience and perfectionism meant that everything she did was done slowly. On my first visit to Ware Hall-House after her death, I heard a story that showed just how slowly that could be.

I was told it by the coalman, who turned up to make his usual delivery, not knowing that Auntie May had died. We told him to leave the fuel anyway and, after he had tipped it into the bunker, he stopped and smiled.

'I must tell you this tale about Miss Savidge,' he said. 'Once, when I came a few years ago, I saw her bent over a huge oak beam – it must have been an eight by eight – and she was trying to cut through it with a bow saw. She was really struggling. I told her I knew someone with a chainsaw that would cut it like a knife through butter; I could ask him to pop round, if she'd like. She said she'd rather do it the old-fashioned way, thanks – the way they did it in the old days, when the house was first built. When I came a fortnight later, she was still cutting it. The fortnight after that, the beam was still on the bench, and when I came through the gate, she picked up her saw and made the final cut. I reckon she timed it so I would see it!'

Our first sight of Auntie May in Wells was almost as dispiriting as our last visit to her in Ware. The new setting she had chosen for her house was beautiful. Wells is a pretty little seaside town with a working quayside and Auntie May's building plot was tucked behind The Buttlands, an elegant village green framed by Georgian merchants' and sea captains' houses and a couple of historic pubs. But when we opened the gate in the wall, the contrast with the rest of Wells was dramatic. There was Auntie May, surrounded by heaps of beams, bricks, doors, windows, floorboards, peg tiles, piles of lead piping, bits of old furniture and other oddities that she hadn't been able to bring herself to throw away. Try as I might, I just couldn't imagine that Humpty Dumpty of a house ever being put back together again – and Auntie May didn't have all the king's horses or all the king's men to help her. I tried to look enthusiastic and optimistic but, inside, my heart sank. The task looked overwhelming. She had got a local builder to lay the foundations and drains before she had arrived; she had recruited a few local fishermen who had agreed to help her move the bigger beams when they needed moving. Apart from that, she was determined to do it all by herself. Tony spoke for both of us when he said we would be happy to give whatever help we could, but Auntie May politely made it clear that she didn't want it.

Still – at least she had somewhere weatherproof to live: the old caravan, with the words 'Blue Lady' painted on the side. She didn't invite us in, but Tony and I stole a glance through the windows. It was so crammed with boxes of her possessions that we wondered how she managed to move about. But we could also see a little cast iron stove, and a glass-domed oil lamp, and a sink, and a table with a typewriter on it and a bed that served as a sofa . . . and Tony spotted an old Elsan chemical toilet in the tumble-down flint outhouse at the far side of the site, so we knew that Auntie May had everything she needed to survive – apart from comfort. It seemed terrible to leave her alone in such circumstances, but that's how she wanted it and there was no arguing with her.

The rebuild was also slowed down by the size and position of the site. The plot was big enough for the house and a small garden, but there wasn't enough space to lay out and sort out all the building materials – most of which had to be on-site from the start. Auntie May had to spend a whole year organising and pulling the nails out of the beams of the frame, moving them from one pile to another, and then moving those piles so that she had space to lay out the next. This was further delayed by the need to have help lifting the heavier beams, and the people she called upon (and paid) to help weren't always able to come when she needed them. The sorting was made even more difficult by the rest of the salvaged materials that were stored there. Auntie May (and her occasional helpers) had to work round stacks of tiles, bricks, doors and windows, door frames and window frames, fireplaces, floorboards and glass. In a normal building project, these things are delivered as they are needed, not all at once. A further complication was that access to the site was narrow and limited. Hemmed in on three-and-three-quarter sides by other gardens, the only way in was by a 4ft-wide gate – and to get to it, you had to go down a narrow lane and then up a narrower alley. (You still do.) When the time came for new building materials to be delivered, they had to be dumped well beyond the boundary and carried up a steep slope.

As if all these obstacles weren't enough, May was also hampered by her conscientiousness as a correspondent. She never left a letter unanswered, and she received lots – many of them from complete strangers. Every time her story appeared in a newspaper, a magazine or on television, more would arrive. Most writers didn't know her postal address, so they made a stab at it, assuming that the post office would know who they meant and where she lived: 'Miss May Savidge, The Blue Lady Caravan, Wells, Norfolk'; 'Miss M. Savidge (who is rebuilding her house), Norfolk'; 'Miss M. Savidge, Mediaeval Hall-House, Wells-next-the-Sea, Norfolk'. They all got there – even one in an envelope that shows that it went to Norfolk Island first.

Strangers wrote to express admiration and gratitude – they congratulated her on her spirit, wished her good luck and thanked her for making a stand against 'progress'. Several sent money. Many offered help. Some asked for it. She got a fair few letters from people who clearly weren't quite right in the head. She answered them all, though sometimes her replies were several months late. As I came upon these letters when I was going through her papers, I found myself wondering what it was about Auntie May that made people feel able to reach out to her with such warmth and trust. As I read her replies to them, I could see that their instinctive affection for her was well placed.

May 14th 1970

Dear Miss Savidge

I must first beg of you to forgive the liberty taken in writing this letter to you, but your spirit has amazed me <u>with admiration, to have your home moved</u>.

I give thanks to my God for being able to offer good References re business and private character. For serious reasons over the loss of my mother (a London nurse) when I was very young – 6 years old – I never married. <u>My mother died</u> in the service of the sick, in London hospitals.

Well, to cut a long story short, I decided some years ago to buy a form of modern living caravan, but <u>I now have to move it</u> – after it has been in the area for 7 years.

I just wondered if you would have a bit of land (at the back of your new home) <u>to offer at a Rental</u>.

However, whatever you think at receiving this letter, would you very kindly forgive me for the liberty taken in directing it to you . . .

Yours sincerely

B— D—*

---

* I have changed this name and that of other people who wrote to her when they were down on their luck.

Ware Hall-House
Water Pit Lane
Plummers Hill,
Wells-next-the-Sea
Norfolk.

25th August 1970.

Dear Mr. D——,

Thank you very much for your letter of 14th May; I would have answered sooner, but have been so terribly busy getting things under cover from the rain, and trying to find things, after the removal of all the bits and pieces of my little house from Ware, to make way for a roundabout and new road. We overran the date, so it was all a rush.

Was sorry to hear that you have to move your caravan, which you have made your home, after seven years. Unfortunately, there is not enough space on this site for a caravan, and the Council would not allow it anyway; they have given me permission to live in one in my garden while I am re-erecting the house, but the permission is on a one year basis, and is for myself and my dependants – my cat and dog.

There is a privately owned caravan site just near here, in Burnt Street, Wells-next-the-Sea, where some people seem to live all the year round, and others come for summer holidays. The other site, which is run by the Council, is just near the beach, and is for holidays only; all the caravans have to be brought away and stored for the winter. I do not know if it is possible to get a single site anywhere around here, but you could write to the Wells Urban District Council and enquire, if you are interested in this area as a place to live.

Hoping you will soon be successful, and thanking you for your good wishes,

Yours sincerely

May Savidge

Formerly of Monkey Row, Ware, Herts.

I found one exchange of letters particularly moving. It shows the quite extraordinary lengths Auntie May was prepared to go to in order to help total strangers, even at the most critical time of her project:

The Daily Telegraph and

Morning Post

Fleet Street

London E.C. 4

Mrs. Savidge,

Monkey Terrace,

Wells,

Next-to-Sea,

Norfolk.

July 13th, 1970.

Dear Mrs. [sic] Savidge,

I have received the enclosed rather pathetic letter, from a man who is at present a prisoner in Wandsworth Jail. I also enclose a copy of my reply to him, from which you will see that I have been most careful not to give him the slightest impression that you would look favourably on his application.

I hope however that you may agree with me that it would have been extremely unkind on my part to neglect his letter entirely.

Yours faithfully,

T. F. Lindsay,

Assistant Editor.

Peter Clark, Esq.,   *The Dailing Telegraph and*
H.M. Prison,   *Morning Post*
Heathfield Road,   *Fleet Street*
Wandsworth,   *London E.C.4*
London S.W.18.   *July 13th, 1970.*

Dear Mr. Clark,

    Thank you for your letter received here on 9th July.

    I have been glad to send this on to Mrs. Savidge on your behalf, but of course you will understand that I have no idea whether she would be able to use your help – or indeed whether she needs any help at all.

    Yours faithfully

    T.F. Lindsay,

    Assistant Editor.

The letter that the *Telegraph* forwarded was handwritten on prison issue paper:

H.M. Prison,
Heathfield Road,
Wandsworth,
London S.W.18.
[undated]

Dear Sir, This is a letter From The above name, And No. mentioned. So my name is Peter Clark. You will wonder, why I am writing to you, well I'll explain my reasons for it. I was reading your Paper, the daily Telegraph dated Tuesday July 7th – 1970. And I seen a Photograph of a woman her name is Miss May Savidge And that she is going to start re-assembling her 500-year-old home in wells Norfolk. So Sir I write to you And ask you if you would be kind enough to send this letter on to Miss Savidge at her Address as I would like to give her a help to build up her house. As you can see by this letter that I am in prison, but I am due for discharge this month July 27th.

So Dear Miss Savidge I write this letter to you in the hopes that you will let me help and work for you in building your house. I can do all building jobs, So when I saw your photo in the paper, I thought I would better ask if you would kindly let me help, And work for you, that's if you want me. I am a good worker Miss Savidge, And I am sure that you will be pleased at me. I have also worked on farms, And done all other kind of work. I know I am in Prison for a little silly mistake I made, But now I have Payed for the mistake And I will soon be coming out, so I want to start life again, I am not to old I am only 49 years old, I know that it is very hard for me, when I come out of Prison As a great many firms will not give me a job or work for them, when they know where I have been, so I ask you miss Savidge, would you really like me to work and give you all the help with building your new home. I do hope you will say yes to me And miss Savidge if you think that you can spare a few little minutes of your time, will you Please write me a little letter, I don't know if you will be angry at me writing this letter to you, But I hope you wont be miss Savidge, But I think you are a kind woman, And understand. Also will you write to me here miss Savidge my name And number And address is at the top of the page. I see by the photo in the paper that there is plenty of work to do on building your house up again, But as I have stated Id be only too pleased And willing to help And work for you.

So will you Please be ever so kind and write letting me know miss Savidge.

Yours faithfully

Peter Clark

Ware Hall-House
Water Pit Lane
Plummers Hill
Wells-next-the-Sea
Norfolk

18th July, 1970

T.F. Lindsay, Esq.,
Asst. Editor,
The Daily Telegraph and Morning Post,
Fleet St., London, E.C.4.

Dear Mr. Lindsay,

Thank you for your letter of 13th July, ref. TL/R, enclosing one from Mr. Clark, and a copy of your reply. I have written to him, explaining that I cannot afford help, which is why I am doing practically all the work myself. Have also enclosed the "Situations Vacant" pages from our two local papers; as he has done farm work, and will be free in time for the harvest, he may be lucky. Am glad he is trying to find work, and would certainly not ignore his letter. If he cannot get a start somewhere, he may drift again.

Perhaps you would like to make a note of my address, in case you ever need it again.

Yours truly
May Savidge, (Miss not Mrs.)

Ware Hall-House
Water Pit Lane
Plummers Hill
Wells-next-the-Sea
Norfolk

18th July, 1970

Dear Mr Clark,

Thank you for your letter of 7th or 8th July, which reached me, via the Daily Telegraph, on Thursday, 16th. I am glad to hear that you will soon be leaving Wandsworth, and looking for work. My difficulty is that I cannot afford help: that is why I am doing practically everything myself. By this method, I reckon I can re-erect this little house more cheaply than buying another one, as well as saving a very interesting old house.

The foundations, water and drainage were done by a small local firm, and were finished before I arrived here, with all the timbers and tiles, etc. Two fishermen, who helped to unload one of the lorries, have already agreed to come along for an hour or so, if any of the timbers are too heavy for me to move. There is not a great deal of work for people in this area, and some of them go to King's Lynn or to Norwich, and come home at week-ends. Even before I came here, I had received a letter from an elderly carpenter and joiner, asking for work, but I have not been able to do anything for him, either. If I had plenty of money, it would be different, but having to move at all is a great expense, whether I bought another cottage, or re-erected this one. I've never had much money, as my father died in 1921, just before I was 10 years old, and there were no pensions in those days, except for war widows and orphans. My Mother's Father had been killed when she was three years old, so there was no help from that side of the family. No doubt, it was this background that first made me tackle the odd jobs at home, like carpentry, that a father usually does, and I have learned a good deal since those early days.

As you have done farm work, and will be free in time for the harvest, I wondered if you would be able to get work in that line, for a start. The fruit growers seem to need pickers. Am enclosing the 'Situations Vacant' pages from our two local papers, the Lynn News and Advertiser, and the Dereham & Fakenham Times, known as the Journal.

Another possibility is a job where week-end work is necessary, as I understand that many people refuse jobs where they cannot get Saturdays and Sundays off, every week. Perhaps you would let me have an address that will find you in the future, in case I hear of anything.

Good luck in your efforts, and don't let the difficulties get you down; as my Mother always used to say, "Worse troubles at sea".

Yours truly,
May Savidge (Miss)

Ware Hall-House
Water Pit Lane
Plummers Hill
Wells-next-the-Sea
Norfolk

16th August, 1970

The Governor,
H.M. Prison,
Heathfield Road,
Wandsworth,
London S.W.18.

Dear Sir,

On or about 8th July, 1970, a prisoner, Mr. Clark, having read an article in the Daily Telegraph, 7th July, about the re-erection of my little house to make way for a roundabout and new road, wrote to me, via the Daily Telegraph, asking if I could employ him, as he was due for release on 27th July.

In reply, I explained that I could not afford to employ anyone, but said that I would let him know if I heard of anyone who could offer him work.

A faint possibility has now come to mind, but as I do not know why Mr. Clark was in prison, or what sort of man he is, I wondered if you would be so kind as to let me know, in strict confidence, something about him, please; what he is like, and especially if he has any tendency to violence, as the person of whom I am thinking, who needs someone to do some work, is older than I am, and lives alone, but is better off financially.

Am enclosing a stamped addressed envelope, and would be very glad of your advice.

Yours truly,

May Savidge, (Miss).

•

H.M. Prison,

Heathfield Road,

Wandsworth,

London S.W.18.

Please address any reply to THE GOVERNOR *and quote JDW/LH*

17 August 1970

Miss M Savidge

Ware Hall-House

Water Pit Lane

Plummers Hill

Wells-next-the-Sea

Norfolk

Dear Madam

Thank you for your letter of 16th August. I regret that I cannot be of any assistance as Clark was discharged from prison on 27th July and his whereabouts are not known to me. I would add that, in my opinion, Clark would not be suitable to work for the person you mention.

Yours faithfully

Governor

•

I spent countless hours reading through the letters May sent and received. Sometimes, I would decide to take just a quick look in one of her correspondence boxes, only to find that the next time I looked at the clock, a whole morning or afternoon had passed. Unlike her diaries, in which she recorded every detail of her project in tightly written notes, her letters were open and chatty – even when written to complete strangers. She wrote as she spoke: as I sat at her desk in the great hall, I could hear her telling her story in her own voice.

> *Ware Hall-House*
> *Water Pit Lane*
> *Plummers Hill*
> *Wells-next-the-Sea*
> *Norfolk.*

18.11.71

Dear Mr. Purdy,*

Thank you for your letter of 12th Nov., regarding the re-erection of my little medieval hall-house from Ware, Herts. I was very interested to hear that you are preparing a thesis on the Restoration and Preservation of Buildings, as one of my reasons for tackling this job was the thought of all the buildings which have been destroyed unnecessarily in the past, and those which are likely to be in the future, if people do not <u>do</u> something about it. One fact that the destroyers forget is that overseas visitors expect to see some old buildings, when they bring their much-needed currency to our country.

---

* Mr Purdy was a student at the Leicester School of Architecture, who had read an article about her in *The Architect & Building News*.

The article in the "Architect and Building News" was more correct than most reports of this move, though I do know of at least two <u>older</u> buildings in Ware, though they are both larger. Since the article was written, I have spent a year sorting all the timbers, etc., after spreading bricks over about half the garden for the purpose; I also had to remove thousands of nails before I could make safe piles of joists, etc. There was no time to remove nails before I came, which was a pity, as it would have been easier to load the lorries. I had some help to move the heavy timbers, and also a carpenter for 4 or 5 weeks, to get the base plate in position. This is a replacement; as you will know, base plates were laid on the earth, with no foundations, so we found only short lengths of the original one. Am now busy doing up some of the lower joists, before erection, and am <u>trying</u> to get some wooden pegs or dowels, which should be made from riven oak, not sawn oak, (for fixing the joints) – hope I do not have to make them by hand, as it would take so long.

You probably know that other houses have been moved, but by groups of people I think. Various friends said that I ought to write up this move, so I have kept notes, and there are endless letters, also photographs etc., but I am not sure what sort of details would best suit your purpose. You are welcome to come here, if it will help you, though the house is no higher than the base plate at present. Water Pit Lane is an old walled footpath, without a name-plate, off Plummers Hill, which is off the S.W. corner of The Buttlands, – a green, (with large trees around it) where by Henry VIII's orders, the local men and boys practised archery, for the defence of the realm. I usually go shopping on Tuesday and Friday mornings, and seldom go out otherwise, except to take my dog for a walk, as I am too busy.

Good luck with your work, anyway.

Yours sincerely,

May Savidge, (Miss).

After our first, discouraging visit to see May in Wells we had talked about her often over the next few months, and although we didn't speak to her – she had no telephone then – we exchanged several letters. Meanwhile, we had plenty to think about in our own lives. We were a long way from finishing the renovations to The Nook and I was pregnant with our second child. We, too, had four walls to rebuild. Auntie May had been to see our cottage during the renovations some years before – and much later it struck me that maybe watching our amateur building had given her the idea that one doesn't need to be a professional builder to renovate a house. When Daniel was born in October 1970, Auntie May sent a letter of congratulations and a gift. We wondered how she was getting on, but with another new baby to look after, the thought wasn't foremost in our minds. She wrote that she would have loved to come and see us, but she felt unable to leave the building site unattended until the house was up and could be secured. We resolved to visit her there as soon as we could.

In the event, our second visit to Auntie May's new home took place in the spring of 1973, nearly two years after she had first moved in. I remember the occasion well. We were looking forward to showing off our little family and seeing how near Auntie May was to finishing her project. She met us at the gate and led us up the steep path to the level part of the plot on which the foundations had been laid. 'As you can see, I have made a lot of progress,' she told us. But we couldn't see any at all. To us, the site looked exactly as when we'd last seen it. The progress, Auntie May explained, was in sorting out the piles of materials that the delivery men had offloaded willy-nilly. She had removed all the thousands of nails that had been left in the beams, and then restacked them according to the numbers that she had painted on them before they had been taken apart. The north, south, east and west timbers were now in their respective positions. The next job was for the base plates to be remade and fixed to the foundations. She had found a local carpenter who had agreed to do this, and he was going to start work 'very soon'.

So, the project had moved on a little, even if it didn't look like it. But at this rate, May would never get the house finished. Once more, we offered to come up and help; once more, she refused. Then events overtook us, as Tony's job took us to Scotland. We didn't want to go. We'd only just finished renovating The Nook and we wanted to enjoy it. Tony was an engineer and was then working for a vehicle instrumentation company. He was a gifted designer and his employers wanted to loan him to a tachograph firm in Dundee – to make the first British 'spy-in-the-cab' devices that a new European law required to be fitted in lorries and coaches. At first he refused to relocate, but they kept coming back with promises of higher pay and bigger incentives until we finally gave in. We moved to Dundee in 1974 and we didn't see Auntie May until we came back south two years later.

By then, Auntie May had – with the help of a couple of casual labourers – got the scaffolding up and the main frame of the building erected, and she had found a man who had agreed to do the infilling with brickwork. But he disappeared after a fortnight, so she had started to do the bricklaying herself. This would have been a difficult enough task for a professional bricklayer, for the spaces between the beams were irregular. Auntie May had no experience of bricklaying, but was determined to lay every single brick absolutely perfectly, so progress was pitifully slow.

Over the next few years, we made a point of visiting Auntie May with the children during their summer holidays. Each time, we would set off hoping to find the house nearly finished; but each time, we arrived to find that little had changed since our last visit.

There was always a hand-printed sign on the gate that said 'IF DOG IS IN GARDEN, PLEASE WAIT OUTSIDE UNTIL I COME'. The dog always was in the garden, but we would go in anyway. Whether the dog barked or not, Auntie May would know that someone had arrived, because she had rigged up a Heath Robinson arrangement of strings, wires and pulleys that connected the gate to a home-made bell hung on one of the beams of the house that would clank away when the gate was opened. She was always pleased to see us, but would never let us do anything to help. 'Why is it all taking so long?' our children would ask.

It seemed to us that going through Auntie May's garden gate was like entering CS Lewis's wardrobe: the world behind the gate didn't have lions and witches and fauns, but it did seem to have clocks and calendars that worked at a different pace. Every time we saw her, she would tell us how she had been waiting for months for one tradesman or another to turn up to do something without which the project couldn't move on. She pottered quietly along doing such tasks as an increasingly frail and elderly woman could manage. Meanwhile, nature began to hide those carefully arranged piles of beams, pushing nettles between them, and winding the floorboards in ivy.

CHAPTER FOURTEEN

Onwards and Upwards

In which Auntie May describes her progress in letters
to her numerous friends and admirers

Then, when we visited Auntie May in the summer of 1977, we saw
some real progress. The roof timbers were in place, and were
covered in felt and battens. The ground-floor brickwork was
finished. The window frames were all in place, even if they were
not yet glazed. At last, it seemed possible that all the bits and pieces
she had brought from Hertfordshire might one day, once more, be
put back together to make a house. But it was to be two more years
before the tiles were on the roof.

But though progress was slow, the tone of the letters May wrote
in the 1970s was breezy and optimistic:

Ware Hall-House
Water Pit Lane
Plummers Hill,
Wells-next-the-Sea
Norfolk.
16.6.74

Dear Pauline*,

Thank you very much for your letter of 11th: was glad to hear that you are coming up this way on holiday, and shall be very pleased to see you both . . .

Only the frame of the house is up so far, – it took me over a year to sort out all the bits, and put them in different heaps in the garden, with bricks underneath to keep them off the ground; also had to remove thousands of nails, which were in the way. Then I got a bit of help, to get the base-plate (a replacement) down on the foundations, which were done before I arrived. After that, I started on repairs to the timbers; the lower ends of all the vertical ones had suffered from having no damp-proof course, – no foundations, either, – so I have had to join pieces onto them. Nothing about this house is rectangular, either horizontally or vertically, so every join takes a bit of working out; it is fortunate that I was on aircraft jig-and-tool drawing during the war, there are very few right-angles on an airplane, either. Last September, two strong young local men came in their spare time and got the frame up – the main timbers, anyway, – the ones that have tenons at both ends, so cannot go in afterwards; there are still several smaller ones to go up, and some replacements. I did start bricklaying in November, until the frost made it awkward, then I did a lot to the hedge, as my new dog kept getting through it; it took me a great deal of time. The land drops away steeply on the other side, so I managed to get enough pipe to go all the way round, and wired wire-netting on to it, and filled in the gaps below. Some of the pipe came from a malting demolition here, and there were a lot of bricks there, so I had a load, which of course included a lot of rubble, but bricks are quite difficult to get now, and very expensive, and I am likely to need extra ones. As one cannot drive to my gate, the load was tipped up in Plummers Hill, and it took me over three weeks

---

* I have not been able to trace Pauline's surname. She appears to have been an old ICI colleague.

to get it all in by hand. However, I'm now dealing with windows, so as to be able to get on with the bricklaying again ...

She sent a letter around this time to a Mr and Mrs Huttlestone, who – I guess – were among the many strangers who heard or read about her, called at the site to wish her well and became life-long friends and correspondents:

> *Ware Hall-House*
> *Water Pit Lane*
> *Plummers Hill,*
> *Wells-next-the-Sea*
> *Norfolk.*
> *17.11.74.*

Dear Mr. and Mrs. Huttlestone,

Thank you for your letter and the lovely photos; I think they are very good indeed, and was surprised to see the one of Sasha* standing there so quietly, after the way she had been barking ...

Am very sorry indeed to have been so long in writing, but there are so many letters in the queue, and I try to spend the daylight hours outside on the re-erection job. Having no electricity makes writing etc more difficult in the evenings; I've fixed up a small mirror to reflect the light onto the paper – sometimes I have to use the front lamp off the bicycle to help out. The Calor gas is all right over the sink, but gives a poor light in this part of the caravan, so I use an Aladdin lamp, but the only safe place for it is at the opposite side of the cabin. The Calor gas is on that side, too.

It was so nice to see you both, and I was so glad that the weather stayed fine for you and that you enjoyed the scenery, etc. There are

---

* Candy had died and been replaced by an Alsatian bitch, Sasha.

some miles of coast and country around here, where wild birds can be seen; about 30 miles of the coast is protected by the National Trust etc. I've had quite a lot of visitors, including BBC-tv, but it rained all that day; they were not after a news item, but are doing a series about people who have done something entirely different after retiring or having to give up work for some other reason. They did a bit of recording here and said they would come again later on. As well as the rain, the Water people were using a pneumatic drill nearby, so the BBC could not have done a proper 'take' anyway. The idea of the series seems to be to encourage people not to sit down and get bored and miserable, but to find out ways of doing whatever they have in mind, including learning new skills. Some folks get really despondent when they give up work. Incidentally, the pneumatic drill cut through my neighbour's gas pipe; she had a meal in the oven, and was resting – not feeling very fit after a car crash – and later on she found the meal still uncooked; the Water people had not found out whose pipe it was.

The rain has been pretty bad this Autumn, hasn't it? I keep covering up parts of the job with polythene, but the strong winds drive the rain in underneath at times. However, I'm progressing bit by bit, and hope we don't get too much snow.

Hope you are both keeping well; kindest regards to all, and I look forward to seeing you again next year, I hope. Thank you again for the photos . . .

Yours sincerely,

May Savidge

I came across another reference to May's lighting problems in a charming exchange of letters with the company that had manufactured her ancient paraffin lamp:

Ware Hall-House
Water Pit Lane
Plummers Hill,
Wells-next-the-Sea
Norfolk.
25th Nov. 1974.

Aladdin Industries Ltd.,
Aladdin Building,
Greenford,
Middlesex.

Dear Sir or Madam

No. 11 Mantles.

For some time, I have been trying to buy some Kone-Kap mantles,
Ref. No. L.146, for use on my No. 11 Aladdin Lamp, and am getting
worried as I am now using the last one of my little stock.

Will you kindly let me know where I can obtain some more,
please?

Please find enclosed a s.a.e. for reply,
Yours truly,
May Savidge (Miss).

Ware Hall-House
Water Pit Lane
Plummers Hill,
Wells-next-the-Sea
Norfolk.
19.1.75.

Mr. J. N. Thurgood,
Chairman & Managing Director,
Aladdin Industries Ltd.,
Wester Avenue,
Greenford,
Middlesex/ UB6 8UJ

Dear Sir,

Thank you very much for your letter of 11th December, ref. JNT.ME.336, regarding the supply of mantles, etc. I was surprised to hear that the last No. 11 was sold in 1929; it says a lot for its quality, though this one was not in daily use between 1949 and 1969: even so, at 45 years or more, it is almost half-way to becoming an antique, and still working perfectly. I first came into contact with Alladin lamps in a country house in 1923, but I do not know when they were made. Have now bought a new one, to use when my No. 11 Mantle collapses.

Yours truly,

May Savidge (Miss)

Another letter that caught my attention was to Rusty and Nargesh Rustomji, who lived in Bombay, India. I recognised the name from one of the calendars May had kept. Rusty had given it to her as a present in 1923 – she had known him since she was twelve.

Ware Hall-House
Water Pit Lane
Plummers Hill,
Wells-next-the-Sea
Norfolk,
England.
NR23 1ES
16.3.75.

Dear Rusty and Nargesh,

This was meant to be a Christmas letter, but I get so "snowed under" with letters and form-filling; I sent off the cards, etc., and hoped the air-letters would overtake the ones going abroad, but I am still floundering, partly because it is difficult to see, with the oil lamp in the only safe place . . .

Re-erecting this house still takes all my daylight hours, except for shopping, etc. Usually in the winter, snow or hard frost would drive me indoors, to get on with letters or other indoor jobs, but this year has been exceptionally mild, so far; there were summer flowers out in January – the wild plum hedge started to bloom, too, but I don't suppose we shall get any wild plums from those flowers. I feel obliged to get on with the house as fast as possible, partly because I have only temporary permission to live in the caravan in the garden, and have to apply each year for a continuation: another reason is that the timbers will deteriorate if left lying in the open too long. I don't think that I am being unnecessarily careful with my repairs to the timbers – you see, the frame has to stand up by itself; there was no brickwork, originally, – that went in at various times afterwards, and if the timbers rotted at all, or were cut away, the brick walls held the place up. But having taken it all apart, for transport, one cannot do the brickwork first, because one cannot tell where it has to go until the frame is in position. It isn't as if the frame were rectangular, or even straight – and it fits

175

together so tightly, with mortises, tenons and oak pegs, that it can't be persuaded to go anywhere except in the right place.

With so many upright timbers to be avoided, I suppose any proper bricklayer would think that the job was too fiddly; I did mention it to four or five, but no one came, so I started trying the bricklaying myself; I had done a bit before. However, a good deal of last winter and spring went in doing jobs to the hedge, as my dog would keep going through it, which could be very dangerous, if she reached the road. The ground beyond the hedge falls away steeply, so it is difficult to block the base, as the earth between the actual bushes slides down the bank, too: it was a long job.

Am bricklaying again now between the showers; the bricks are not all the same size, and are various colours, – both due to having been added at different dates. Shall be very glad when the job is finished and the furniture out of storage again, but it is an interesting job to do, and is one little effort against the destruction of so many old buildings, which people do like to see: also, with such a housing shortage, it seems silly to destroy this one and occupy one that someone else could live in . . .

Very best wishes to you both,
Yours sincerely,
May Savidge

May always replied to the letters she received, but her in-tray was always piled high and her reply to Rusty and Nargesh was by no means the only one to be sent a year late. Many of the letters she wrote begin with apologies for the delay, followed by a detailed explanation of why she hasn't been able to write sooner – as in her Christmas 1977 letter to Gordon Moodey, secretary of the East Hertfordshire Archaeological Society, whom she had known since 1954:

Ware Hall-House
Water Pit Lane
Plummers Hill,
Wells-next-the-Sea
Norfolk NR23 1ES

Christmas, 1977.

Dear Mr Moodey,

Thank you so much for your letters of last December, April and November, and for the Newsletters — 40, 41, 42 & 43, which I was very pleased to receive. Am extremely sorry that this letter is so late — have only just written letters to Australia and India, which should have been there by Christmas. All the year I thought the roof would be on by Christmas; earlier in the year I thought I would have moved in by then, — so Christmas arrived and I was prepared for it. During April, two young builders did a bit of work here, but disappeared — three times — by then it was the middle of June. They had talked about getting the roof on "now", but it seems I was only a stop-gap — I suppose they found other work nearer home, in a nearby town. I began enquiries for a little help to get those 24 joists in my bedroom ceiling/attic floor into place; they are tenoned into two tie-beams, which have to be lifted out, the tenons put in, and then replaced, so the job __had__ to be done before the roof was started, as the principle rafters are tenoned into the tie-beams. At the end of October two local young [men] came and did the job, in one day — we used a little chain pulley to lift the tie-beams. Later, they put up four pairs of principle rafters, collar beams, etc., on odd days, but they both have other jobs — one of them goes to sea, fishing — so they cannot spare much time. Meanwhile my efforts to find someone to help with the roof have come to nothing, but I think someone is coming in January! — not the best time to be doing roof work — hope we finish before the March winds arrive — we

have had at least three gales since this part of the roof went up,
already.

    Was very interested indeed in the change of attitude of the planners
regarding old buildings. I'm sure the elected Council people – and
others – would have been surprised if they had known the number of
people who used to express regret at the demolition that was going on;
but these people only speak to people like me, and not to the powers
that be – they have the idea that nothing can be done about it – it just
has to be, because somebody or other says so . . .

    Yours sincerely,
    May Savidge

I found it heartbreaking to read that May had thought she
would have been able to move into the house by the end of 1977.
More than seven more years would pass before she could finally
do so.

Meanwhile, she received a constant stream of visitors, many of
whom turned up unannounced. They all found the note on her
gate about the dog. When the postcard the note was written on
became worn and faded, Auntie May wrote out another. I found
five copies among her papers. I expect there were more. I also
found a note from a Mrs Fellows, whom May knew from their
days in the Ware St John Ambulance Brigade. It was dated 14
September 1978 and written in pencil on the back of a raffle ticket,
the only paper Mrs Fellows had in her handbag at the time. It
offers good wishes, tells May she has had a hip replacement and
says that she recently 'caught a glimpse' of Auntie May on TV –
when the BBC regional news programme *Look East* had come to
report on her progress.

Ware Hall-House
Water Pit Lane
Plummers Hill,
Wells-next-the-Sea
Norfolk NR23 1ES
17.9.78

Dear Mrs. Fellows,

Thank you so much for your little letter; I was very disappointed indeed not to have seen you on Thursday. I was there somewhere, and expect I was inside the unfinished house — my work bench is there. There is a wire attached to the gate, which rings a bell close to the bench; my dog barks at nearly everyone who goes by along the footpath, so I only go to the gate if the bell rings. The path is a handy route to the Orchard Caravan Site in Burnt Street, so most of the people who go by are holiday-makers, and if the children find out that I have a bell, they keep ringing it and running away, — so I dare not mention the bell on the note on the gate. I tried to word the note so that people who wanted to come in would open the gate, but be prepared to close it again if the dog rushed towards it. There is an extension wire from the bell to my caravan at the far end of the garden, as I cannot hear the bell in there, but it requires the gate to be moved a foot at least, as the wire is rather long, so sags a little.

It was good to know that you are getting about again, after that hip operation, but I was very sorry to think of the pain you must have suffered before you had it. There are some wonderful things done to joints now-a-days, — I seem to remember drawing some of the plastic 'bones' when I first went to I.C.I.; I think the idea was fairly new, then.

If you are in this area again, I would be ever so pleased to see you. Just at present, I do all my shopping on Saturdays, as I am expecting someone to come to do the outside plaster around the upper half of the house for me. I shall do the inside later; it will be a more fiddly job, as I want to show all the timbers on the inside. Someone else is going to put the tiles on the roof – I shall help. After they have both finished here, I shall revert to my old shopping days – Tuesday and Friday mornings; I have a padlock and chain inside the gate, but leave a note on it if I have to pop out; I also lock the gate at night, with all those clay tiles and other things piled up on the site.

. . . I am now making a window for the gable end, facing the gate – you may have seen a tower of light-weight scaffolding there. The original window had three oak mullions mortised into the collar-beam halfway up the roof, so was not intended to open; the replacement did not open either, but I felt that it ought to, at that height, in case it is ever needed as a fire escape, so I am copying the original window, but in an oak frame, with hinges. Working on old oak takes me a long time, as it is so hard; I must finish this window and some other pieces before the plasterer can do this south wall, but the other three walls are ready for him, so I hope he comes soon; he was coming in August . . .

Kindest regards to you all, and hoping you will soon be quite fit again,

Yours sincerely,

May Savidge

In December 1978 the publisher Jay Landesman Ltd wrote to suggest that Auntie May's story might make a book, to be written by a ghost writer. They had in mind 'a light-hearted account of the difficulties and the way you overcame them – an entertaining book based on your illustrations'.

Ware Hall-House
Water Pit Lane
Plummers Hill,
Wells-next-the-Sea
Norfolk,
NR23 1ES

12.1.79

M/s Jenny Wright,
Jay Landesman Ltd.,
159, Wardour St.,
London, W. 1.

Dear M/s. Wright,

Re-erection of Small Medieval Hall House.

Thank you for your letter of 6th Dec., suggesting a book about the re-erection of this little hall house, which was in the way of a new traffic roundabout at Ware, Herts., and which you read about in the Evening Standard of 1st Dec.: Christmas and other happenings have delayed my reply, I'm afraid.

First, I must say that there were several mistakes in the article, and that I have not yet moved into the house. I had some help with the roof, and the man has promised to come back and put the tiles on; I shall help. Another man is going to plaster the outside of the upper part of the house; I shall do the inside later, as it will be a fiddly job, making dozens of separate panels, so as to show all the timbers on the inside. At present, I am working on the outside doors, and a few windows, etc.; neither of these men is likely to come until the weather is good.

This house had been threatened since 1953, just because it was old, so I had plenty of time to decide that I wanted to keep it, long before the roundabout was even thought of. Ever since the dismantling began, (in Sep. 1969) people have asked me to write about the whole job, so I made notes each evening about what we had done: after I arrived here (in June, 1970) I even typed out some of these notes, as I had been asked to give a talk about the move. Have also taken a lot of photos, and these and notes have come in handy at times, during the re-erection, quite apart from being a basis towards a book.

When I have moved into the house, I shall finish the typing and proceed from there. I have always been fond of writing and never thought of a "ghost" writer. During the years, many visitors have asked questions, so I have a good idea of what interests them and what they want to know. My writing would not be quite the approach you suggest, as that would disappoint people – they want to know much more than that – but it would certainly be light-hearted and with illustrations.

Am sorry for the delay – there is so much to cope with,

Yours sincerely

May Savidge.

If Miss Wright wrote a reply to this letter, I have not found it. I did, however, find a large number of letters written to May by people who had read about her continuing efforts in articles published in the national press. A Mrs Hillsdon wrote to share her memories of the baker's shop that had occupied one half of the building when it had been in Ware.

Buckinghamshire

May 24th 1979

Dear Miss Savidge,

I was fascinated to read the article in Woman magazine about the removal of your cottage from Ware to Norfolk, as many years ago I was very familiar with the building.

As a child I spent many happy holidays staying at the bakehouse in Baldock Street . . . I remember the building well, especially standing in the old bakehouse watching the bread come out of the oven. My bedroom was the one with the window looking out over the yard of the public house next door and the floor was always warm from the oven beneath. The floor of the landing upstairs was most uneven . . .

I can see the shop now — with the sponge cakes in a glass case, the cottage loaves, the doughnuts, the varying sizes of fruit cakes and above all the sticky buns — two of which I was given each morning for lunch. It was a great privilege for me to be able to serve in the shop on occasions . . .

I hope your venture will soon be completed and I wish you many happy years in your cottage in Wells-next-the-Sea.

Yours sincerely,

G.N. Hillsdon (Mrs.)

One of many strangers to write to congratulate May for her efforts was a man who had been kept going through a family crisis by her example:

London,
3rd October 1979

Dear Ms. Savidge,

Some weeks ago my son became very ill, and during the long hard struggle before he died last Spring, the story of your courage and determination was one of the things that helped sustain us. The newspaper cutting telling of your tremendous achievement in rebuilding your house has been on my bedroom wall all these months; many times I intended to write to you, but somehow I never seemed to find the

time, the peace & writing materials all in the same space. But now I
have time to thank you for the inspiration you gave the children and
myself when we most needed it . . .

As May approached the tenth anniversary of her move to Wells, the tone of her letters became noticeably less optimistic. There is an air of resignation about them – though she is still cheerful enough in herself, despite all the difficulties and delays. On 17 February 1980, she wrote to her old school-friend Peggie Hutton:

Ware Hall-House
Water Pit Lane
Plummers Hill,
Wells-next-the-Sea
Norfolk NR23 1ES
17.2.80 for
Christmas, 1979.

My dear Peggie,

This was supposed to arrive for Christmas; am so sorry it is so late, but my lamp keeps going dim – too dim for writing by – so I am more snowed under with letters than ever; shall be glad when I get electric light again. The man who was going to put the tiles on the roof of the house has not been here for almost two years; the man who was going to plaster the upper part of the outside has not done any work here since Dec. 1978, though he did call recently, after I had 'phoned. He does have back trouble, having injured his back years ago, and they all seem to be very busy. So I plod on alone, with the jobs.

Yours affectionately,
May Savidge

CHAPTER FIFTEEN

Becoming a Celebrity

In which Auntie May appears on television and receives —
and replies to — more and more fan letters

Stories of Auntie May's progress continued to be published in
newspapers and magazines at home and abroad, and in the spring
of 1980, national television came knocking, as a BBC television
crew arrived to make a short film for the evening news programme
Nationwide. I've got a tape of it. It's a little work of art. It paints a
subtle picture of Auntie May's gentle but determined character and
records exactly what she had so far achieved. Looking at it now, I
am struck by how derelict the Blue Lady appears. It had been pretty
tatty when she first bought it, but now, after she has lived in it for
more than ten years, the paint is peeling off and the weeds are
growing right up to it. May looks old and tired. She says very little
and speaks very softly in reply to Sue Cook's questions.

'May is a gentle, solitary soul; she spends her every waking hour
working,' says Miss Cook. That was true enough.

'How long did you think it would take?' asks Miss Cook.

'Well nothing like as long as this, but it's difficult to get help,'
Auntie May replies.

'Wouldn't you prefer to live in a nice warm modern house?'

'No, not really, not when you can live in an interesting old house. I don't want something silly and modern – that doesn't strike me as nice at all!'

'Isn't it a bit cold and lonely here?'

'No! I've got the dog and the cats. I'm used to being on my own – I've been on my own for donkey's years.'

'Have you ever thought about giving up?'

'No! Not likely!'

The camera watches her climbing a scaffold tower and slipping in some fillets of brickwork. She moves slowly, but purposefully. There is a strange little scene in a local pub, in which half a dozen cheerful regulars are shown chatting to Miss Cook. We don't hear what they say, but in a voice-over, Miss Cook says that there are mixed feelings about Miss Savidge in the town. The scene gives the impression that Auntie May is somehow not connected to the people of Wells – she is an outsider. There is an interview with Mr Terrington, the builder who put down the foundation slab for her. He is obviously full of admiration for Auntie May, but he does gently point out that he has never been convinced of the wisdom of the project. He says he suggested that he could have had a nice new house built for Auntie May to move straight into back in 1970, but that wasn't what she wanted at all. He says that her first idea had been to bring the frame of the house up in one piece, slung under a helicopter, but that was obviously never going to happen. Auntie May is asked how long she thinks it will be before she has finished work and can move in. She says she doesn't know, but that once the roof is on, and there are no more drips coming through, it should be quite soon. Mr Terrington is asked the same question and he says that, if she doesn't get help, he really doesn't see how the project can ever be finished during her lifetime.

In 1981, more publicity – an article in the *Guardian* and a news item on national television – moved a number of strangers to write to May. The *Guardian* piece, published on 5 January 1981, was accompanied by a photograph of Auntie May at her most bag-lady-like, wearing a woollen hat under a headscarf, and clutching an overcoat to herself with mittened hands. The text misspells her surname and rechristens her 'Edna'. Nellie thought this might be on account of an Edwardian actress of that name, but I suspect that the writer had subconsciously likened Auntie May to the scruffy and lonely misfit played by Patricia Hayes in the TV play *Edna, the Inebriate Woman*. In the photo in the *Guardian*, Auntie May stands by a tumble of brambles and old timbers in front of the house, which looks decrepit and tatty – more like a building falling down than one being rebuilt.

> Although now aged 69, she insists that the time she takes is immaterial. 'It is only a fraction of the life of the house, which is how I like to see it,' she said. 'I want to live here, of course, but I want others to be able to live here after me. That is what is important.' There are some who feel she will never finish her tasks. Miss Savage [*sic*] has no date in mind but is sure that one day the construction will be complete.

It is clear that the author of the piece is not quite so confident.

One of many to send in money was a woman in London, who enclosed a cheque for £100:

January 7th 1981

Dear Miss Savage,
   In front of me I have a cutting from The Guardian with your photograph and story and I cannot let another day pass without

telling you of the happiness and humility with which I read and re-read it.

Thank you for showing us, in these sad, bewildering times, what courage and quiet determination to achieve a selfless vision can do.

Please accept the enclosed cheque towards the re-building of Ware House — if it advances by only half an hour the completion of your task, I will be very proud . . .

PS Please do not give up a moment of your precious time to answer this; it needs no reply.

Poor people sent in offerings, too. In March, a woman from Colchester wrote May a letter of support that began: 'Please find enclosed one antique nail. My husband got it when he was in the building trade, now retired in ill health. I admire your guts immensely, it spurs me to get jobs done myself around my modern bungalow . . .' Another letter received about this time came from a Belfast student, who enclosed a £5 note, and apologised for not being able to afford to send more.

Many of the letters May received thanked her for saving her ancient house for the nation:

Yorkshire.
April 28th 1981

Have just seen on TV the programme about your 'moving house' to Wells-on-Sea. I think you're marvellous. Yours is the spirit of independence and creative imagination that once made Britain great. I pray that the programme may result in really useful offers of help, so that the beautiful house for which you care so much may be completed this year, and you may enjoy many years of living in it. You are building part of the nation's heritage, not just a place for you

*to live. I'm the same age as you were when you started the project,
and can imagine just a little of what you must have felt . . .*

I read these letters in the dusty, cluttered house after May's death,
squashed between upturned chairs and bedsprings. It was a
compulsion. To peek into those cream-coloured folders made me
feel part of May's life – and often moved me to tears.

May received hundreds of unsolicited letters like these and
replying to them took time. A huge backlog built up, in which
letters to her family and friends got caught up. In July of the
previous year, she received a tear-smudged aerogramme letter
from Nargesh in Bombay, telling her that Rusty had died. She
finally got round to replying to it just over a year later.

*Ware Hall-House
Water Pit Lane
Plummers Hill,
Wells-next-the-Sea
Norfolk,
NR23 1ES
England.*

21st June, 1981.

My Dear Nargesh
    *Thank you very much for your letter of last year; I was so very,
very sorry to hear your sad news – it must have been a terrible
shock to you, being so very sudden, although a wonderfully peaceful
way to leave this life. I hope you are getting used to loneliness a
bit now, although I know only too well that nothing fills the gaps:
keep[ing] busy, and keep[ing] your mind occupied helps, I
find, and also one gets tired enough to sleep . . .*

Am very sorry indeed that this letter is so very late; it is not due to heartlessness — I owe hundreds of letters, some of them official ones — electric light would help a great deal — I get so tired, especially in a dim light. My paraffin lamp went wrong for about a year, and I have never managed to catch up since. There are boxes of letters piled up in the caravan which is so full that it is difficult to find anything. Last year I had more visitors than ever, mostly complete strangers, and as the caravan is so far from the gate, I took the typewriter into the unfinished house; had to fix a polythene tent over it, as the roof dripped rain: I tried to type with a hurricane lamp hanging up . . .

Recently, a good builder has been helping here, and the roof tiles are now on, so at last, there are no drips: he has done some other work here, and has promised to come back and do the downstairs floor, so I hope to be able to get my furniture out of storage soon. Meanwhile I am doing various jobs, mainly carpentry — repairing windows, etc., and cutting down the growth in the garden, before the weed seeds blow into other people's gardens. Before Christmas, I bought cards and stamps, but that is about as far as I managed to get — I was just too tired to get them written and posted, so must try to make amends now, while there is more daylight, and before the builder comes back; I get very tired trying to keep up with him, as he is much stronger and younger than I am, but a marvellous help: I often fall asleep over my evening meal . . .

I do hope you are keeping well, and hope to hear from you when you can manage it; there is a lot to see to, when living alone.

All my good wishes and deepest sympathy,

Love from,

May

Please forgive the long delay.

Things took another significant turn in 1982, but unfortunately, it wasn't a turn for the better. The firm that had stored Auntie May's possessions for the past eleven years ceased trading and she decided to have all her stuff delivered to the house. Thereafter, the house was jam-packed with clutter. Nellie had told me that May had always been a compulsive hoarder, but only now did I realise quite how much she had accumulated over the years. When she had lived in Monkey Row, most of it had filled the neighbouring two-storey workshop, which had been as big as a family house. Now, it filled Ware Hall-House to bursting.

When we visited her in the summer of 1982, we found the Blue Lady caravan crammed with boxes. Cardboard cartons covered the bed, stacked right up to the ceiling. There was no room for anyone to get in, let alone live in it, and Auntie May had moved into the house. But things were almost as bad there – there were only three small spaces in which she could stand or sit. One was in the front room, where she typed her letters on a tatty antique desk; the second was an old chair and table in the great hall, in which she slept and ate. There was a small area in front of the butler's sink in the room that had originally been the bakery. The only other space not covered by ceiling-high packing cases was occupied by the dog basket – which visitors had to stand in.

And yet Auntie May had made some progress since we'd last seen her. She had put down floorboards upstairs and in the attic. But she had immediately covered them – again, ceiling-high – with her possessions. The ground floor wasn't quite so full, but only because Auntie May had left narrow passageways between the vast piles of boxes and clutter. There was no way much internal rebuilding work could be done while all that stuff was there – but then, for the time being, that didn't matter, for there was still much to be done outside.

In December 1982, a BBC *Look East* producer wrote to Auntie

May to ask if he could bring a TV crew to film an update on her progress since his last visit in 1978.

> *Ware Hall-House*
> *Water Pit Lane*
> *Plummers Hill,*
> *Wells-next-the-Sea*
> *Norfolk,*
> *NR23 1ES*
> *9.12.82*

Mr. Ian Masters, BBCtv Look East,
St. Catherine's Close,
All Saints Green,
Norwich,
Norfolk, NR1 3ND

Dear Mr. Masters,

Thank you for your letter of 6th December. I was surprised to hear that some of your viewers had written to ask how this job is going.

When you came in 1978, I think that the roof and the upper part of the outside of this house would have been covered with roofing felt; the man who was going to do the plaster on that upper part did not come back, nor did the man who was going to finish the roof; I did not think I would be safe on the tile battens at my time of life. Other men said they would come, but did not; at the beginning of 1981, however, a different man came and did the outside plastering, and put the tiles on the roof, and did a few other jobs as well. He is very good and very busy, but he had a bit of time to spare last Christmas, and came and did a bit to the downstairs floor – (2" cement screed on the concrete),*

---

* Auntie May was 71.

and more of it on some Saturdays. Before he had finished, however, the firm where my furniture was in storage closed down, so as the roof is watertight, the furniture, etc., is here now. It is good to see it again, and better for it to have some air, but it is rather in the way.

The same man says he will come again some Saturday mornings, and do a bit more to the floor, – then the plumber could come – so now I do all my shopping for the week on Fridays; therefore, Mondays to Thursdays would be the best time, if you wish to come; I am here all day, usually doing the woodwork jobs, as cement work is a bit heavy for me . . .

Yours sincerely,

May Savidge (Miss).

A letter to May's cousin, Alan, and his wife, Joan, describes the progress that was made on the house in the spring and summer of 1983:

Ware Hall-House

Water Pit Lane

Plummers Hill,

Wells-next-the-Sea

Norfolk,

NR23 1ES

4.9.83

Dear Alan and Joan,

Thank you so much for your letter of 1st August, and for the cheque which you very kindly enclosed: it is very good of you and is much appreciated. Yes, I am still very busy on this job – the fine weather helps sometimes, but is rather overpowering – I see that you are not keen on the heat, either. Fortunately, there is usually a bit of breeze on this coast . . .

In May the plumber came and fitted the kitchen sink; there is one in the caravan, but I have to carry the water there, so having my old sink and a proper tap is a real treat. He is coming back to finish the bath, etc. Just when he was able to come, I started having trouble with one leg, which I had knocked, and had to rest it a lot, but it has just cleared up, at last, so I am getting on with windows, etc. Have also got some floorboards for the attics — only one had a floor, before; I want to take some things up there, as, since the furniture came out of storage last year, there is a bit of clutter on the downstairs floors.*

Am enclosing a plan of this house, as you suggested — am not re-erecting the Tudor chimney stack, as it was not there in the first place, and blocked the cross-passage completely, as you can see from the two shallow hearths which used to be of the inglenook type and were back to back, with two more hearths upstairs, with brick four-centre Tudor arch fireplaces. The upstairs bathroom will be where the huge chimney stack was (ventilation in the roof) so that the landing can run full length. The extra bathroom, downstairs, is in most of the former pantry. Am still using ladders indoors, but can do the stairs in the winter, being an indoor job; I have to barricade the first ladder, as my dog can get up it, but can't get down again . . .†

Love to all,

May

It was about this time that another film crew arrived. This one was led by the young Polish director, Witold Stok, accompanied by his wife, Danuta. They had picked up the story in the article published in the *Guardian*. Something about that article fired the Stoks'

---

* This is something of an understatement!

† There were three ladders in the house at this time. One was riddled with woodworm and carried a notice: 'Warning: for cats only'. When I saw this on our visit in the summer of 1982, I had to suppress a childish giggle.

imagination and Witold wrote to Auntie May asking if he could come and talk about making a film. She agreed. She never sought publicity, but she never turned it down. She felt that it was just plain wrong to destroy our architectural heritage, and the more people that were shown it could be saved, the better.

Auntie May mentioned the Stoks' visits in the letters she wrote to thank us for the Christmas presents we had sent her in 1981. We realised she must have been having difficulties completing the project, because she didn't find time to write it until the end of the following October:

> *Ware Hall-House,*
> *Water Pit Lane,*
> *Plummers Hill,*
> *Wells-next-the-Sea,*
> *Norfolk NR23 1ES*

> *26.10.82*

Dear Tony & Christine, Polly & Danny,

Ever so sorry this is so late for Christmas, again; I was just getting on with letters etc., last winter, when Mr. S., who had put the tiles on the roof, had a bit of spare time so came back and did some of the downstairs floor – putting the 2″ screed on top of the concrete base. It is a heavy job for me, especially as the sand has to come into my garden in wheelbarrow-loads up from Plummers Hill; he has a youth helping him now, and one pushes, and the other pulls a rope tied to the front of the wheelbarrow. I had to keep moving things out of the way, indoors, so that he could do a bit and let it dry and set properly; also had to keep my dog off – the cat's paws did not make much of an impression.

Before Mr. S. had finished, however, the firm where my furniture was in storage decided to close down, so as the roof is now watertight, I have all the furniture here. It is nice to have it, and better for it, too, as warehouses do get damp, but it is rather in the way; there are so many boxes of things piled up everywhere. Mr. S. is coming back sometime, to do more of the floor, then the plumber would come – he has been to see the job – a different man, as the other plumber never came.

Meanwhile, I'm very busy indeed with woodwork, etc., also moving things to make more space, – and now, to add to the chaos, I've mislaid my address books, – a real problem – I can remember <u>some</u> addresses, but not all, and the postal codes.

Thank you very much indeed for your lovely presents and cards; I am so sorry not to have written sooner – I do wish I could keep up with letters, etc., but I owe so many, and I am trying so hard to get this house finished enough to be able to invite people to stay – there are enough bedrooms – at present, two beds are covered with apples! – a good crop, but a lot of maggots.

Must get this posted; love to all, and I do hope you are all keeping well,

Yours affectionately,

Auntie May

XXXX

P.S. More delays – before I'd managed to wrap up the parcel, the members of the little Polish group have been again, doing a bit more to add to their film – there wasn't much space for our feet among all the boxes, etc. We were looking through my photos of this job at various stages, and came to the photo of you all: they may wish to include one of them – I hope you wouldn't mind.

Love from

Auntie May

•

The final cut of the Stoks' film was 25 minutes long, and it was first shown at a conference held at Ruskin College, Oxford, on 10 March 1984. Auntie May didn't see it until its second screening, at the Wells Centre on the following 5 May. I wish she had told me about it: I'd have loved to be there with her. But I only heard about it in a letter she sent me some months later, and I didn't get to see the film until after she had died. I found a copy of the programme of the Wells showing among Auntie May's papers and what I read made me want to get a copy of the film:

> This creative documentary captures the rhythm of the woman's lonely and endless task. She saws, chisels, hammers, builds, survives Spartan conditions yet, as her voice-over discloses, she never loses hope. But twelve years after its dismantling, the house still remains unfinished . . .

I wrote to Witold Stok and he sent a charming reply along with the videotape. It is a curiously affecting little film, in which Auntie May is shown pottering about at all sorts of tasks amongst her clutter, while her old clock ticks slowly in the background and her radio carries the BBC news. One item is a report of the death of the one-time Soviet president Leonid Brezhnev. Another describes the wedding of the Prince and Princess of Wales. Auntie May doesn't seem to be listening – the point seems to be that these events are happening in a world in which Auntie May plays no part. While the commentator rattles on about the glamour of Lady Diana's wedding gown, Auntie May pulls on a battered overcoat as she prepares to go out. The contrast is pointed, but not patronising. She is presented with admiration and respect.

I later learned that not everyone in the audience at the Wells Centre screening had responded positively. It must have been a strange evening. Years later, Witold and Danuta described it to me and I read about it in a book I found among Auntie May's possessions. Its author, Patrick Wright,* devoted a whole chapter of *On Living in an Old Country*† to the story of Auntie May. He describes seeing Auntie May sitting at the front of the audience, dressed in her all-weather topcoat, woollen hat and scarf – even though it was a mild, spring day. She had brought a bunch of honesty from her garden to give to the Stoks. (Wright wondered whether it was her way of saying that she hoped their film would be an honest account.) Most people in the audience treated her protectively – someone took her by the arm to help her to her seat, which was quite unnecessary, as she was still capable of climbing ladders and scaffolding unaided; but then, she was in her seventies and she looked frailer than she was.

After the film, the audience was invited to discuss what they had seen. One or two of them addressed a question to Auntie May, but most people talked about her as if she wasn't there. A rather snooty woman said that one Miss Savidge in Wells was enough, thank you; any more, and the value of local property would be dragged down. A couple of women argued that the film wasn't feminist enough: why was it called *Miss Savidge* – what had her marital status got to do with anything? One man said to his neighbour that Auntie May was a fly old bird who had been milking public sympathy for years. Someone else said that if everybody in the room were to give up just one afternoon a week

* Patrick Wright is one of the hundreds of names recorded in Auntie May's loose-leaf visitors' book. He came on 6 May 1984. The Stoks had last signed it in March 1983, leaving notes of farewell and thanks on 24 May.

† A new edition of this book has just been published by Oxford University Press.

to help her, the house would soon be finished and she could be comfortable at last. There was a murmur of general approval and several people shouted: 'Hear, hear!'

I don't think any of these people understood Auntie May at all – not even the kindliest of them. I wondered how many of them really understood the film. I think it's beautiful. It shows Auntie May as someone detached from the concerns of modern society – and though the audience didn't realise it, the comments they made confirmed the view of the Stoks.

Another interesting point that Patrick Wright makes is that the conference at which the film was first shown had been about patriotism. Later, when I delved into the records that Auntie May left behind her, I could see what the Stoks must have seen: that Auntie May's determination to save her house sprang from her love of her country, of the history that had made it what it was and the inheritance that she wanted to pass on to later generations. Early in the film, Auntie May says something particularly revealing: 'I was a bit fed up. They keep destroying everything.' She speaks of the enemies of those values as 'they'. I think that's why the Stoks called their film *Miss Savidge*. The title suggests the contrast between the faceless, soulless and unseen authorities that have taken over England, and an individual who has sacrificed everything to stand in their way. That individual has a name. It is Miss Savidge. It's Auntie May.

CHAPTER SIXTEEN

'Getting a Bit Old Now . . .'

In which Auntie May finds the going increasingly difficult

On 30 August 1985, the *Dereham & Fakenham Times* revisited May's story under the headline 'May, 74, works on at rebuilding old house'. It reports that 'the major building work has been finished for some time', but that 'Miss Savidge has not yet moved out of the caravan that has been her home since 1970'. What the reader isn't told is that apart from the fact that 'brick floors are being laid', the project is not much further on than it was two years earlier: 'Miss May Savidge, now 74, continues to climb up ladders and scaffolding with great agility while she continues to tackle her present task of replacing windows.' She is still having problems 'finding someone to replace leaded glass'.

The upbeat tone of the report did not reflect reality. The project had stalled. Much of Auntie May's energy was now being spent on patching up jobs that had been finished earlier. Days fill with trivial tasks, like repairing mop handles, mixing tiny quantities of mortar to plug gaps in the walls, or struggling to remove rusted-in screws. Her diaries contain increasing references to time spent repairing rips in the PVC sheeting that covered the window frames, none of which yet contained glass. On the day that she had made her final move to Wells, she recorded the occasion triumphantly in her diary; I expected to find a similarly upbeat note of her final move from the caravan to the house. There isn't one.

I scoured and rescoured the 1985 and 1986 diaries, but there is no record of her moving into the house. She does refer to taking her meals there, and it is clear that, from the autumn of 1985, she and the animals are spending their nights there, too, because the first entry of the day is often a note that she has had to clear up the 'puddles' and worse that her Alsatian, Lorraine, has left in the cross-passage of the house.

I puzzled about this. It didn't seem to make sense. When we visited Auntie May in the summer of 1985, she was obviously living in the house, where there was now a working WC and bath – though it was also clear that she was sleeping in her chair in the great hall downstairs and not in a bed. There were tiles on the roof. She told us that she had found a very helpful local plumber, Mr Jarvis, who had renovated and refitted the old taps, water heater, bath and basin she had brought from Ware, and had built the walls of the bathroom itself. Then I read that *Dereham & Fakenham Times* article again:

'I have started eating meals in the house because I am worried about the dog knocking over the gas lamp in the caravan,' said Miss Savidge. 'I can't get permission to move in until the windows are fixed.'

Maybe that's why she didn't mark the move in her diary – in one sense, she never actually made it. I think she believed she wasn't allowed to and was worried someone in authority would turn up and condemn the place as unfit for human habitation and force her to live in a 'council bungalow'. I am sure that was the main reason she didn't want anyone from the surgery to enter the house. I wonder whether to begin with, at least, she persuaded herself that she hadn't actually moved in, as she wasn't sleeping in her bed. From this time on, the first diary entry of the day notes which chair she had dozed in the previous night – and the stool or stools on which she rested her legs. After a while, each entry is the same: 'Old chair, corded stool, canvas stool.'

Our visit that summer wasn't a happy one. When Tony rang the bell at the garden gate, Auntie May didn't appear for ages, so we let ourselves in. This was a mistake: her Alsatian, Lorraine, was loose and ran at Tony, who was holding a present that we had brought. I can't now remember what it was, but he needed two hands to carry it, which meant that when the dog went for him, he couldn't fend it off. It bit him in the leg, and wouldn't let go. May was mortified, but she did point out that the note on the gate said visitors should wait to be let in. The atmosphere remained tense for the rest of the day.

We could see that the project was drifting. It was as if Auntie May had lost sight of the bigger picture and had her head down to concentrate on the minor tasks that were arising day by day. Not all of these related to the building. It seemed to us that much of her energy was expended on looking after the dog, which seemed to be like a cuckoo in the nest, demanding attention that was needed elsewhere. In the car on the way home, we agreed that if things went on like this, Ware Hall-House would never be finished – and, worse, it might even begin to fall down.

Years later, when I read Auntie May's diaries, I realised that her problems had been even worse than we had imagined – though she records them with no trace of self-pity or complaint. We had been right about the dog – but we hadn't known the half of it. The 1985–1988 diaries are dominated not by difficulties with the house, but by difficulties with Lorraine, the Alsatian bitch she had adopted after it had been found wandering in King's Lynn. May's hope that she would eventually become biddable were not realised. She was never even properly house-trained. For month after month, May records clearing up 'puddles' and fouling in the cross-passage leading to the front door – she had a carpet she would have liked to put down there, but knew that if she laid it, it would only be ruined. Sometimes she had to clear up three or four times a day, even immediately after exercising the dog in the garden. As if this weren't trouble enough, Lorraine wouldn't walk to heel, leapt up at other dogs and several times pulled Auntie May to the ground. People noticed. The kindly Mrs Leftley at the grocer's recommended that she got a 'Halti' leash – a lead and muzzle combined. Auntie May got one, but she still couldn't control the dog. Every time she opened the gate to take her for a walk, there was 'the usual battle' over who was in charge, and Auntie May never won.

In November 1985 Auntie May was on television again. This time, it was BBC1's regional news programme *Look East*. The programme celebrated her move into the house and gave the impression that the project was nearly finished. But this was far from true. There was still no staircase – the first and attic floors were reached by ladder. There was still only a 'builder's supply' of electricity – four sockets on a board in the hallway served the whole house. A single, bare bulb hung over Auntie May's table and chair in the middle of the great hall – which, like the rest of the house, was still packed, floor to ceiling, with all those boxes of Auntie May's stuff. Auntie May cooked and heated water on a veteran Beatrice paraffin stove in a tiny space cleared in the room that was nominally the kitchen.

Auntie May was in, but she still didn't have a telephone. Anyone wanting to contact her had to call in, write – or, as many journalists had done over the years, send a telegram. Tony and I were worried about her health. She had never really been well in all the time I had known her. She suffered constantly from indigestion. Even a cup of tea could upset her stomach: she had to drink it very weak. Over the years, she had worked out which foods troubled her least and stuck to them. There weren't very many of them. She seemed to live on a diet of bananas, carrots, prunes, cheese, biscuits and Kit Kats. On one of our visits, Tony and I battled past the nettles and brambles, and took a walk around the overgrown garden. We found a 5ft pile of what looked like little jet-black twisted sticks – it turned out they were hundreds of desiccated banana skins. Heaven only knows how many bananas she must have eaten in her lifetime. I guess that she liked them because they were easy to chew – she had terrible trouble with her teeth. She also suffered terribly from ulcers on her ankles and legs. She never complained of them, but we knew they were there because we could see the bandages. Sometimes she was in so much pain that she could hardly walk.

The cold can't have helped. The winter of 1985–1986 was bitterly cold. We knew the temperature in the house must have fallen well below freezing, because when we visited in the summer of 1986, Mr Jarvis told us that Auntie May had called him out three times in February and March to mend her frost-blown pipes. The only heating in the house was an ancient electric fan heater that looked like a vintage aeroplane engine. It ran so constantly that its housing glowed red hot and Auntie May was frightened that it would catch fire.

MON: 17.2.86 – Fingers get so cold – otherwise O.K. . . .

FRI: 21.2.86 Up at 7am. Temp. in Great Hall 24°F. at 10am.
L[orraine] puddle & f[ouling] in x-passage . . .

The following Monday, the pipes in the house burst, and while she was waiting for Mr Jarvis, the plumber, she spent her time struggling to get a mattress into one of the bedrooms. There were no stairs in the house yet, so she tried to get it up the scaffolding tower and in through the window, despite the '*ICY E. WIND*'. She failed. A week later, she had another go: *'Tue 4.3.86 'managed to get 4 ft. mattress up to B[edroom]3 and onto bed.'*

In March, Auntie May spent even more time than usual cleaning up after Lorraine, who was suffering from vomiting and diarrhoea. Another way in which the dog – 'That damn dog!' I found myself thinking – was making Auntie May's life even more difficult was by driving away her cats. At this time, she had three: Shelley, Charlotte and Ginger. The only way she could feed them was to climb the ladder to the first floor and put their food in the bedrooms, where Lorraine couldn't get at it or them. For the rest of the time, the dog stayed by Auntie May's side, so the cats wouldn't approach her – and she was reduced to watching them from afar. She compensated for not being able to pet them by making detailed notes of her sightings of them in her diary. One day, the dog managed to follow her up the ladder – and, worse, couldn't get down again. After that, Auntie May had to keep a plank against the rungs when she wasn't climbing them herself.

On 13 June, she received a pleasant surprise in the post: an invitation to a Buckingham Palace garden party to be held on 17 July. Whoever drew up the invitation list must have read about her in the papers, or seen her on the television. The invitation was for Auntie May and a companion. She asked Nellie to accompany her. (Years later, Nellie told me that when May had telephoned her from a callbox to invite her, she had begun by saying that she was calling to ask if she would like to come with her to see the Queen. Nellie, assuming that May had finally lost her marbles, told her to put the phone down, calm down and ring again when she was feeling better. Five minutes later, May telephoned again. Only then did Nellie take her seriously and agree to accompany her to the palace.)

May got herself a new outfit for the garden party: a handsome flower-print voile dress and a white hat with matching gloves. I suppose she only ever wore them once. After her death, I found them all carefully wrapped and stored in her wardrobe. They were like new. The day itself, alas, did not go well. Auntie May admired the gardens and the flamingos, and caught sight of a hat that she thought might have been on the head of the Queen; but then she was so overcome by the heat that she was physically sick and had to be helped to a seat to recover. She was sick again on the train on the way home. Later, she noticed 'patterned lights' before her eyes. Her health was beginning to break.

It was at about this time that we had a family conference and decided we would try to persuade Auntie May to get a telephone installed. Nellie and Bern, and Mies – her Dutch cousin – and Tony and I agreed that we would all slip the idea into a letter, as if it had occurred to us independently. Nellie and Bern would say they were getting old now and finding it increasingly difficult to get up to see her by car. Mies would write to say that it would be very useful for keeping in touch with her in Holland, given that letters take longer to arrive from overseas. I would just say that I thought a phone might be a good way of keeping in touch.

The real reason was that we were all terrified she would have a fall and have no way of calling for help. We all wrote as planned, but unfortunately, she had an answer for us and it was an answer that made perfect sense: a telephone would make her life more dangerous, because if it rang when she was up a ladder or on the scaffold tower, she might slip as she hurried to answer it. We had a rethink and Mies wrote to suggest a cordless telephone – one that she could carry with her. A few weeks later, when Tony and I visited, Auntie May told us that she was thinking of getting a telephone – one of those cordless ones. We bit our tongues and said: 'What a good idea!'

Needless to say, once she was connected, she logged every call she made and received – even the calls that she wasn't able to answer in time. Every time the phone rang or she made a call, she wrote 'phone' in the margin of the diary, beside an entry noting precisely what happened – even if the phone rang only once and she didn't manage to answer it. One of the first calls she received was from Mrs Terrington, who offered to do her daily shopping; and Mr Terrington 'said 'phone if I need help, even during the night! – very kind of them'.

Such offers of help were timely. Auntie May writes that she is frequently tired, and some of what she writes is confused. On the 1986 anniversary of her parents' wedding, she writes '*MOTHER & DAD – 60 years since Dad & Mother got married.*' But it can't be: in 1986, Auntie May was seventy-five years old. It must have been the eightieth anniversary.

During the autumn of 1986, there is little mention of building work in the diaries, but among the handful of telephone calls recorded there is an amusingly inappropriate one from a double-glazing saleswoman:

TU: 4.11.86 . . . 6.15pm. – 'phone – young woman on double glazing etc. – haven't fitted single glazing yet . . .

I laughed out loud when I read that.

The 1986–1987 winter was another ordeal by frost for Auntie May. In January, the temperature plummeted, outdoors and in. On the morning of 11 January, she woke to find the water in two milk bottles she had left on the draining board had turned to ice, cracking the glass, and that the hot-water bottles she had put in the cats' baskets upstairs had frozen solid. Mr Terrington telephoned to ask if she was OK – he had noticed there were no footsteps in the snow leading from her gate. She told him she hadn't been able to get down the path, so had exercised the dog in the back garden. He said that if she needed anything at all she should call him and he'd come immediately. But Auntie May didn't call, she battled on.

MON: 12.1.87 . . . Removed 4″ to 6″ snow . . . & put food for birds – G[inger] puss in B[edroom] 4 – took some food there too. Even pets' food in tins frozen after opening. After garden with L[orraine] I slipped over – had to crawl back to E. door, to get up . . . Later, up to B[edroom] 2 – on stool from bathroom, got 2 nails into top of window frame for a piece of wood in the gap – while doing this, L[orraine] barked – down – E. door – Mr. M. Owen to see if I needed anything – he wrote my 'phone number – gave him 2 g[allon] paraffin container . . . Too dark to finish window piece – hands so cold – down again – more HW bottles for Charlotte.

TU: 13.1.87: Mr M. Owen came with 2 g[allons] of paraffin: £3.20. Mr Leslie IRONS called (Priory Cottage) to ask if I wanted anything – left his card for 'phone no. – I said if he saw a loaf . . .

WED: 14.1.87 . . . SNOW up to top of gum boots – skirt wet . . . Pat Terrington 'phoned – I mentioned loaf – son will come this afternoon to clear path.
Mrs IRONS & daughter (no hat!) came with loaf – small cut loaf.

Abt. 1 pm. – <u>Peter Walsingham</u> – thinks he will run out of paraffin – lorry could not get here Monday so he brought some to regular customers – 1 gallon.

<u>Kevin Terrington</u> came with loaf (large white) . . .

Afterwards, B[edroom]2 – fixed 2 boards (wide T[ongue] & G[roove]) into space at top of window with orange 'Farmer's Glue' – icy wind – fingers very cold – put some wood props to hold boards from blowing in.

During the rest of 1987 there are many days in which she records nothing beyond the time she got up, the state of the weather, her sightings of the cats and the time she locked the gate at the end of the day. The last entry on many days is the word 'Dozed'. There are many nights in which she records things that happen in the small hours – sometimes she is woken by them, but more often she is awake anyway:

<u>Th: 26.2.87</u> . . . 3.20 a.m. G[inger] Puss on bed B[edroom]1 – 3.50 a.m. Garden with Lorraine – no use – (4.10 a.m.) Shelley stayed in parlour. Hardly any sleep (R. leg) – kept having to change position.

She writes down the time whenever the bell rings, but the note is often followed by 'nobody there'. Sometimes children have rung it and run away; sometimes, she is just too slow to get to the gate. Her shopping lists all contain Savlon for her ulcerated legs, and paracetamol for all sorts of pain. She writes that she finds it difficult to walk: her ankles are so swollen that she cannot put on her 'top boots', which 'protect my legs from Lorraine's claws, when she jumps at other dogs'. She has a set of dentures made and fitted. She makes frequent references to tiredness. She notes the deaths of several friends. And on Thursday, 5 March, she gets some bad news:

After 5.30 p.m., 'phone — Mr. M. Owen — just got back from Fakenham and found G[inger] Puss dead in his garage — he wondered whose cat he was . . . I said I thought he'd been living wild for some years — he was so terrified of people — I said he might have got some food elsewhere, as he was only sleeping here — but I think he had given up eating really — plenty of food on landing, but he didn't even touch the milk. <u>Poor puss</u> — just when I thought he was getting used to me . . .

Ten days later, Auntie May heard Shelley making unusual miaowing noises. The next day, she found that she had burrowed under the blankets piled on one of the beds upstairs. She put a hot-water bottle beside her and offered her a little warm milk.

'She cried a few times during the night, but raised her head in response to stroking under the chin. I tried to sleep — (on edge of bed) (she was in the middle) — up after 6.30 a.m. — left her well covered up . . . — about 11 a.m. <u>Shelley was dead</u>. She had come out from under blankets.

<u>*TU: 17.3.87*</u>
Aft[ernoon]. Finished hole and buried my darling Shelley — such a loyal little puss — afraid of other people, so I had thought she was safe here — her twin brother was a friendly puss & he has disappeared & her mother, also friendly, has left me and prefers outside Homestead* kitchen window — Buried Shelley in cardboard box — lying on left side — head to the W. end, so facing the house — her coat looked beautiful — black with ginger mixed in it — white underneath, also lower part of

---

* The name of a nearby house.

face – black sleeves on left front paws – others white – put dark grey
tiles on top of grave – then planted the Cheerfulness bulb in the middle
– the one that she dug up from . . . near ash tree.

Locked gate – after 6.30 p.m.?

V. tired & R. ankle and leg hurting – Dozed.

Auntie May's legs and ankles continued to cause her pain and make it difficult to sleep. On 25 September, when she went to collect her pension in the Station Road post office, she fainted and had to be helped onto a chair; she recovered and went on to Leftley's in the High Street, where she fainted again. The Leftleys took her and her trolley home in their van. A few days later, her GP Dr Ebrill called at the house to see if she was OK. She left the chain on the door and assured him through the gap that she was able to cope. On 21 October, a health visitor called, and Auntie May spoke to her with the door on the chain, while Lorraine made a lot of noise and jumped up at her.

Auntie May wasn't giving up. She was determined not to spend another winter in a freezing house and started looking for a Rayburn cooker to install in the kitchen. That would keep one room in the place warm, at least. But solid fuel cookers need chimneys and the rebuilt Ware Hall-House didn't have one. Before a Rayburn could be fitted, the place needed a flue. Auntie May decided that the short-term solution was to get an electric cooker – but she was stymied here, too, because she hadn't yet plastered the kitchen wall against which the cooker would sit.

Meanwhile, everyone could see that Auntie May was running out of steam. We had seen how weak she was becoming when we had visited in the summer. Tony and I were terrified that she would have a fall and not be found. In the winter, that might mean freezing to death. But for all her medical experience and training, she kept the doctor at arm's length. On one visit, I called the surgery to give Dr Ebrill our phone number, and to let him know that we were doing our best to keep an eye on her. He told me that he understood the problem – he was in fact making regular calls to check that she was OK, though to begin with, she would only speak to him through the letterbox. In 1990, Dr Ebrill told me that it couldn't be long before she would have to accept medical help. 'We are just waiting for a minor catastrophe,' he said.

Tony and I decided we had to do something to help. We telephoned in October and told her that we would be coming up with some Perspex to fit in her windows. It wouldn't be as good as glass, but it would at least make them weathertight. In the event, Tony's work commitments prevented him from coming, but our son Daniel came in his place and we brought everything we needed for a day's work. We also brought up a little electric oven and cooked frozen pizzas in it. We left it behind as a present – though we later found that Auntie May hardly ever used it.

The little oven had been my mother's and I began to realise that my feelings for May were somehow daughterly. I'm sure many can relate to losing a mother – and how the subsequent opportunity to care and look after someone frail brings with it a certain comfort.

Despite all her difficulties with her house, her health and her animals, Auntie May's spirit was not broken. On 7 November, she attended a public meeting in the Community Centre, called by the Campaign to Save Wells Hospital. As soon as she got home afterwards, she typed a letter in support.

Ware Hall-House
Water Pit Lane
Plummers Hill,
Wells-next-the-Sea
Norfolk,
NR23 1ES

7th Nov. 1987

Mrs. E.M. Allen,
Chairman
East Anglia Regional Health Authority,
Union Lane,
Cambridge.

Dear Madam,

Please let me add my note of dismay at the idea of closing *Wells Hospital*. Has anyone thought of the <u>cost of all the extra transport to King's Lynn or Norwich — not only in money, but in lives?</u>

There is already a great deal too much traffic on the roads, and too many accidents, even in good weather: what about fog, ice and snow?

The delays and additional accidents should not be ignored; they all cost far too much.

Yours truly,
May Savidge (Miss).

Later that month, I made another visit to Wells. Horrified by how weak she had seemed on my last visit, I brought her a bottle of multi-vitamins.* Worried about her being scratched and knocked over by her dog, I brought a screw-in spike, set it in cement in the

---

* I found the bottle, unopened, after her death.

garden and attached a long chain to it. Frightened that she would knock over the ancient paraffin lamp in the kitchen, I got an extension lead and rigged up a light bulb there. Up until then, she had only been using electricity to run a single light, her radio and the fan heater, all of which were connected directly to the builder's supply that brought power to just behind the front door. Auntie May, who never did seem to get to grips with matters electrical, hadn't thought of using extension leads and was grateful for the suggestion.

Three days later, Auntie May had more bad news. She hadn't seen Charlotte for four weeks, and when she went into town on Friday, 20 November, she bumped into a Miss Danby, who told her that the cat had wandered into Mrs Pinder's house, where she had been allowed to sit in front of the gas fire. She had accepted a little milk and then curled up in the garden shed for the night. The following morning, Mrs Pinder had found her there, dead. Mr Abel had buried her in the garden. Neither of them had known that she was Auntie May's cat.

Nineteen eighty-seven came to a quiet end. Auntie May spent Christmas and New Year's Day alone, though she was invited in for a glass of sherry – the first alcoholic drink she had had for years – by a neighbour, Mrs Jones, who heard her struggling to post a Christmas card through her letter box.

The diaries for January, February and March 1988 are sparse and patchy. The handwriting wobbles and there is little to record except shopping lists, nosebleeds and polythene windows blowing in and being patched up.

But at the end of April, the diaries begin to fill up again and the handwriting is once again neat and purposeful. I am sure the spring weather must have helped. On 24 April, Auntie May wrote and underlined, twice: 'B2 WINDOW – AT LAST watertight.' That day, some old ICI friends made a surprise visit – one of them was staying in Holt, where, she said, the ironmongers, Bakers, had a display of new and second-hand cast-iron cookers. On Wednesday, 27 April, Auntie May got a lift to Holt and chose a solid-fuel Rayburn. She left a £400 cheque by way of deposit and asked to have it delivered later that summer. Things were looking up.

Over the next few months, Auntie May spent some time plastering in the kitchen, but progress was slow. Reading the diaries, one can see why – she was making up mixes using only a pint of water at a time. A professional plasterer would have used gallons – and, indeed, would have someone to do the mixing for him. She seems to have spent as much time cleaning splashes of plaster from the floor as putting it on the wall. She finished on 15 September and spent the next month moving furniture around so that there was room to get the Rayburn in. Then she telephoned Bakers and told them she was ready for it. They delivered it on 17 October. At the top of that day's page in the diary, she wrote 'RAYBURN at last' and underlined it in red.

But getting the Rayburn working involved rather more than just getting it in. That day, Auntie May telephoned a builder she had been recommended, to ask if he could build her a chimney – he said he was tied up for months. The next day she asked Mr Terrington if he knew anyone who could do it; he said he would ask around, but didn't think she had much chance of getting it started before Christmas. When he called round to take a look the next day, he pointed out that the floor wasn't strong enough to take a brick-built chimney of that height. A few days later, she got the man from Bakers out to ask if they could fit a steel flue instead. He said that they could supply one, but didn't have the men to put it up. Auntie May had her old problem again – finding a builder who could come and do some work.

The days were getting shorter and it looked like Auntie May was going to be spending another winter in an ice-bound house. Armistice Day came round again and she found herself remembering the original event:

FRI: 11.11.88. 70 YEARS. – I remember <u>Ellen Pritchard</u> telling <u>Mother</u> that morning that there was talk of an Armistice – I didn't know what an Armistice was, <u>but it happened</u>.

Christmas came and went. The weather over the New Year was mild. On 12 January Auntie May called another builder for help with the Rayburn. Towards the end of the month he came to size up the job and agreed to take it on.

But he didn't come back. The weather was mild, though, and as winter turned to spring, the Rayburn business became less urgent. On 27 April, Auntie May noted in her diary that it was exactly one year since she had paid her deposit to Bakers of Holt.

She spent a lot of time in the garden that summer, but found it difficult to move about on the uneven ground, even with her walking stick. When both hands were free, she tried keeping her balance by using two garden rakes 'like ski-poles'. It seems to have worked, but I don't think she can have been using them on the night of 29 June:

<u>10.30 p.m.</u> gdn. with L[orraine] – slipped over – took me an hour to get up – earth a little soft from rain – in 11.30 p.m., slightly muddy.

Rereading the diaries now, the words 'if only' echo through my mind. If only we had lived nearer – Tony and I are both such practical people and there was so much more we could have done to help. If only Auntie May had booked her builders in advance, instead of asking for them when she needed them and then politely waiting. If only Auntie May hadn't been so frightened that 'they', those in authority, might force her to move out if they saw the conditions she was living in, perhaps she would have allowed 'them' to help. If only Auntie May hadn't found her elder sister's concern for her so patronising, perhaps she would have let Nellie and Bern do more for her, too. If only she hadn't been determined to keep her family at arm's length; if only, when she said 'No thank you, I'm fine' to us, we had replied, 'No, Auntie May, you're not, and we are going to do something about it'; if only, if only . . . but it was not to be. She was determined to defend her independence at any cost.

The first anniversary of the Rayburn's arrival was on 17 October. Christmas came. The weather over the New Year was dull, with temperatures in the low 40s Fahrenheit. On Tuesday, 2 January 1990, Auntie May managed to get hold of the builder. He said he hadn't forgotten Auntie May's job; he had been busy. In fact, he had nearly called a few weeks ago when he had last been in Wells. He would look out those Rayburn leaflets and come and see her soon. He would ring first, in case she was out. A month later, he hadn't called. She wrote that she had meant to telephone him on Friday, 2 February, but had dozed off.

The weather turned windy. On 26 February, Auntie May noticed that the whole frame of the roof window had been blown out – she couldn't find it in the garden and put roofing felt on the floor of the attic to stop any rain that came in from running downstairs. March turned to April. The garden filled with hundreds of purple and white honesty flowers; the tulips and the white hyacinth came out – but there was no news from the builder. On Easter Monday, 16 April, the yellow marigold rose opened. By the end of the month, the flowering currant was almost over, but the laburnum, the hawthorn and the clematis were in bloom.

The builder did some measuring in early April and, when he had gone, Auntie May noticed that he had left behind his tape. He didn't return in April. He didn't return in May.

In June, Auntie May ordered a garden seat from Platten's DIY shop in Wells. She spent some time clearing a space for it, and otherwise pottering about the garden. She writes the word 'TIRED' after noting small garden tasks. The seat was delivered on Friday, 22 June.

> _SAT: 23.6.90._
>
> _F[ell] a[sleep] in old chair, corded stool, canvas stool._
>
> _Sun & clouds – breezy, windy. 58°F._
>
> _Cut off length of wire (16 SWG) – & bent it – gdn. – curled it around little tree trunk, then locked chain onto it & pulled chain around tree trunk & padlocked it to leg of seat – O.K. All the seats were chained at Platten's D.I.Y. forecourt – and this garden and gate are so hidden. Nice to be able to sit down for a minute out there – legs get so tired (& let me down at times). Better varnish it, or paint it, during a dry spell – Blackbird perching on its back already – better put a duster in polythene bag out there._

At the end of June, the builder reappeared, and told Auntie May that he feared a steel flue might end up costing more than a brick chimney, even with all the necessary foundation work. He would find out more and come back to her.

At 3pm on Wednesday, 12 September, he turned up with his tools and set to work. He cut some holes in the upstairs floorboards and measured the gap where the roof window had been. He said he would make a replacement at home and fit it later. He appeared several times over the next few weeks. On Wednesday, 17

October, Auntie May wrote in capital letters in her diary: '2 YEARS SINCE RAYBURN CAME.'

On 30 November, Auntie May telephoned, and 'asked if there was any chance of getting the Rayburn installed by Christmas'. Christmas was exceptionally windy. One of the plastic windows blew in on Christmas Day. On 28 December, Auntie May's legs hurt so much that she went to the doctor, who prescribed an antibiotic. The winds got worse in January. The word 'tired' occurs frequently in the diary. Auntie May had another serious nosebleed – it lasted three hours, this time. On 1 February, she telephoned the builder. He said he had a couple of jobs to finish, some emergencies – and 'one of three years' waiting'. I can well believe it.

On 6 February, the temperature dropped to 36°F and it began to snow. Auntie May noticed that the kitchen tap was 'almost frozen' and that there was 'some ICE in kitchen'. She went into winter survival mode. She knew what to do.

Filled various water containers, including v. large saucepan – Turned off water at main & downstairs W.C. – up to other W.C. – emptied cistern – down again and turned on outlet to empty all pipes – gdn. To see if it was running O.K. – very slow – thought there would have been a good flow – perhaps pipes are already partly frozen – later, icicle from outlet – also from kitchen tap.

The following day, the temperature dropped to 28°F. Auntie May found that the mop she kept in the cross-passage to clear up after Lorraine had frozen solid. At 12.30pm, the electricity supply failed – and the only heater in the house was electric. She telephoned Seeley's, the electricians. They came, and decided it was an Eastern Electricity job. Eastern Electricity came, and decided that it wasn't.

Auntie May called Seeley's again, and they came straight back — to discover that the fuse in the extension lead had blown.

During the cold spell, various neighbours called to offer help; they brought water, and salt and grit for the path and steps. On Tuesday, 12 February, the temperature rose to 36°F and Auntie May noticed that the mop in the cross-passage had thawed. She had tried to thaw it in front of the fan heater, but it hadn't worked. By Sunday, 17 February, the temperature had risen to 37.5°F and the snow in the garden had gone. Auntie May turned on the mains water stopcock — but it leaked. She phoned Mr Jarvis, the plumber, who said he would come round the next day. He came at 3.15pm, and fixed the stopcock and several other leaks he found, too. He couldn't stop for a cup of tea — he had three more calls to make.

He left at 4.30 p.m. Lovely to have tap water again. V. tired.

Auntie May made some progress in 1991. Mr Jarvis pointed out that one reason the place got so cold was that the kitchen door fitted so badly. He fixed it for her.

Nineteen ninety-one was also the year in which Auntie May finally found someone prepared to make and fit windows with leaded lights. She had first started looking nine years earlier, but the urgency of the task had been overtaken by other priorities. In April, she saw an advertisement for the Thorpe St Andrew Glass Company in the *Yellow Pages* telephone directory. Anybody else would have phoned them up, but May didn't. She sent them a letter, in which she told them the history of her project and offered them salvage materials they might wish to use: 'I have some lead, if that would help, mostly old gas pipes and electrical coverings, also some glass; I also have sufficient "Bantam" scaffolding and some ladders.' I don't suppose many of the glass company's customers made offers like that. I don't imagine many of them felt the need to explain why they needed to ask for professional help, either: 'I do as much of the work here as I can myself, not being wealthy,' she wrote, 'but am getting a bit old now.' She was, in fact, not quite eighty.

The glass man came, measured up and gave May a price. She agreed and that summer, the job was done. By the time he left, all the windows that had originally had leaded lights were fitted and glazed – but there were still several other windows that were just frames covered by polythene. It was twenty-one years since Ware Hall-House had been moved to Wells.

CHAPTER SEVENTEEN

The Beginning of the End

In which despite her failing health, Auntie May clings fiercely to her independence

Nineteen ninety-one was the year in which May's troubles with mischievous boys from the town reached an unpleasant peak. I had known that some of them used to tear off the name card from her gate, or ring the bell and run away. But I didn't know about the more serious incidents until I found her diaries. I found those passages very difficult to read. I still do. She recorded them with her usual attention to detail and with a directness that makes it seem the events have only just occurred. Reading them made me – still makes me – want to rush round to comfort her and to give her tormentors a good talking-to. But I can't. It's another 'if only' to add to my list.

On the afternoon of Friday, 7 June, a boy came to the door claiming that May's next-door neighbour had asked him to cut her side of the hedge. It was an obvious lie. She asked why the neighbour hadn't called round himself. At this, he changed the subject and asked her whether she could lend him £5 – or even £2 – he would bring it back tomorrow. Meanwhile a taller boy appeared, who made Auntie May feel even more physically threatened. She told them both to get out of her garden and shut the gate. They went. 'I have no witnesses,' she wrote. 'There were two of them – they could deny it.'

Auntie May rarely recorded her feelings in her diaries, but her unhappiness is obvious in an entry she made two days later:

> _SUN: 9.6.91 53 YEARS SINCE dear Denis died_ – _Thank God I've met some decent men in my life – can't think what Denis would have said to that stupid boy on Friday afternoon._

Two other boys taunted her on 13 August.

> _Abt. 7.15 p.m. – 2 boys knocked at door – one looking through letter box (10 or 12 years old?)_

> _'Do you want any help? Do you want any shopping?' (At 7.15 p.m.?)_
> _'Have you got any fags?'_
> _'Just one?'_
> _'I don't smoke'_
> _'You do smoke' – cheeky pair – kept saying 'You do smoke' and 'Can we come in?'_
> _Would not say who they were – asked them to go – I wanted to hear 7.20 programme – I mentioned police and telephone –_
> _'You haven't got a telephone – you haven't got a telephone.'_

> _When I closed the door, they got hold of it and shook it as hard as they could – letter box and knocker, I suppose – I told them to go – trespassing – bolted door – parlour, to see what they might do next – they pulled bell wire as hard as they could – Down to gate with Lorraine (lead around rope) – gate wide open – bell wire broken . . . Not a pleasant pair._

That autumn, Auntie May was plagued by a number of other boys who turned up to ask her to sponsor them for charity walks; some brought genuine sponsorship forms, but others did not. On 20 October, one called to ask for sponsorship on a cycle ride 'in aid of the churches'; she gave him £1. When he had gone, Auntie May found a further £8 missing from her purse. Two days later, someone pushed a lighted banger through her letterbox. Two days after that, a bigger one was set off right outside her door. When she came out to investigate, she found a boy making 'red Indian' noises at her over the gate.

Auntie May's entry for Christmas Day is depressingly sparse:

_38°F. – No wind. Some sun._*

By January 1992, Auntie May had turned to Mr Jarvis the plumber to get the Rayburn installed. He was putting the finishing touches to it one day when a gang of boys broke the padlocks on her gate and forced their way into the old Blue Lady caravan. An antique teapot was stolen. In ordinary circumstances, Lorraine would have seen off any intruders, but she had fallen ill and wouldn't leave her basket. On 16 January Auntie May found the padlocks broken again and four boys in her garden. She telephoned the police. It was a bad day, followed by a worse night. She sat up, nursing the dog and worrying that the boys might come back under cover of darkness. Then, at 2.10am, 'Dear Lorraine died.'

It was all getting too much. In the diary for the rest of the month, Auntie May was frequently 'tired', 'very tired', or 'tired and hungry'. On Monday, 27 January, Nellie telephoned and

---

*When I read this, I remembered a very different Christmas May had recorded ten years earlier, when she climbed up the scaffolding at midnight on Christmas Eve to take photographs of the stars.

repeated a suggestion she had made several months earlier – that Auntie May should find a flat and move out of the house for the rest of the winter. Auntie May said that wouldn't be necessary.

On the afternoon of the following day, Tuesday, 1 February 1992, she wrote:

> *Mr J. lit the Rayburn fire!!!!* Lovely. Wood and some 'Phurnacite' *from small bunker by caravan.*

It was three years and eight months since she had paid the deposit on the Rayburn at Bakers of Holt.

Things were looking up. The ever-helpful Leftleys found Auntie May a new dog and collected it from the RSPCA in Norwich. It was a mongrel, called Muttley.* The man from Thorpe St Andrews Glass came to fit the leaded windows. The stolen teapot was recovered from an antique shop. The boy that had taken it was given a police caution. The policeman dealing with the case said to Auntie May: 'That should get those boys out of your hair,' and, for a while at least, it did.

But Auntie May's health was failing. The handwriting in the diaries begins to deteriorate. At 10.30 on the morning of Friday, 24 April, she lost her balance, fell and cut her face. It took her over an hour to get back on her feet. She wasn't strong enough to take Muttley out for walks; indeed, she was 'too wobbly' to go out at all. She found it difficult to keep the Rayburn alight – the fire-box needed riddling and she hadn't the necessary strength. Friends and neighbours rallied round. The doctor called and the health visitor made regular visits. Pat Terrington suggested that one of her

---

* Auntie May couldn't have known that it had been named after the sniggering hound in an American children's cartoon series – she never owned a television.

employees, the ever-kindly Sylvia Yarham, might be prepared to help by taking the dog out a couple of times a week and, in the event, she came much more frequently. Sylvia and Pat also brought bits and pieces of shopping that Auntie May needed in addition to the order that Leftley's delivered. Pat agreed to be named as a contact on the form Auntie May filled in to get an 'emergency pendant' – an alarm worn on a necklace that sent a call for help when pressed. Heaven knows, she needed one. She didn't have a staircase in the house and was still getting upstairs by using a ladder:

SUN: 4.10.92.
Aft[ernoon]
Up to B[edroom] 1 etc. Very difficult at TOP of ladder – nothing to hold on to, & I have to crawl. V. difficult to get up. Tied rope around banister rail to hold when coming up . . .

Tony and I kept in touch with Auntie May by telephone. We had been rather preoccupied with planning our daughter Polly's wedding that summer. We tried to persuade her to come, but she said she was too frail and bent, and reading her diaries later, I can see how true that was. But she did send a present: '2 pr. Pillow cases in wedding paper – & card of tide at W. end of Wells beach.'

Nellie was keeping in touch by phone, too. At 'about 8.40pm' on 23 October, Auntie May called her to thank her for the latest cheque she had sent to cover the cost of the telephone. She also thanked her for sending two wedding photographs and Nellie told her all about the event. But the call left Auntie May feeling downhearted. In the 439th of her 440 diaries, for the first time, a shadow of deep sadness falls across the page:

I've got <u>Emergency Pendant</u> (Nellie knows a man who has one) – it
is attached to phone –
   <u>Rayburn</u> O.K. – & <u>dog</u>. –
Yet she still wishes I would get a bed-sitting room somewhere –
Give all this up?
(I don't try to influence her life) So depressing – I would have to give
up – (she would like me to give up) – DOG, EMERGENCY
PENDANT, 'RAYBURN', HOUSE, GARDEN, FURNITURE,
ETC. – W.C. on both floors.
HOW WOULD I GET THERE? Have not been out shopping since
Easter –
I spent most of my <u>early life</u> in <u>other people's homes</u>; now I have
<u>freedom,</u> and I've <u>worked hard</u> for it.

She was clearly deeply upset by Nellie's suggestion, even though I am certain it was only meant for the best. The idea preyed on her mind. On 29 October, she wrote: 'Still trying to forget <u>Nellie's</u> <u>BED-SIT</u> wish (23rd OCT.)', and when Nellie telephoned on Friday, 6 November, Auntie May wrote 'she did not mention bed-sitting room this time'.

•

Auntie May's eyes were getting worse. She kept seeing coloured lights and patterns before them, and on 7 November it got so bad that she 'had to stop trying to write'. She was also having problems with her pendant alarm: she kept leaning against it and setting it off by mistake. On Sunday, 8 November, after she pressed it by accident for the seventh time, she made a protective cover for it out of 'A soup packet & a clothes peg'. On 21 November, she mislaid her keys and spent the next two days looking for them.

On the morning of 3 December, she pressed her emergency pendant button by accident again. At about 3.15pm, Sylvia came to walk the dog, bringing Auntie May a present – a pink and red scarf that her mother had knitted for her. Mr Jarvis, who had been working on the stairs, riddled the Rayburn before leaving at 5pm. Auntie May put her empty milk bottles on the doorstep at the east end of the house.

Diary number 440 ends half-way through the following day. Mr Jarvis is finishing off the stairs. She gives him a cup of coffee at 11am. She has lunch at 1.15. At about 1.30, she telephones Leftley's to place a shopping order. The entry is at the bottom of the last page of the book. For a few weeks, she carried on writing increasingly illegible notes on the back of dog tin labels, but if she copied them into a final diary, I haven't found it.

I do, however, have a good idea of what happened in the last few months of her life, because it was witnessed by many visitors to Ware Hall-House. Christine Abel and Sylvia Yarham continued to keep an eye on May and help her look after Muttley; the Terringtons called in to make sure that all was well; the Leftleys continued to make grocery deliveries and personal visits. On most days, Mr Jarvis was there, doing various building and repair jobs, and generally doing his best to make May comfortable. Having fitted the Rayburn, he had realised how much she had come to rely on him and had taken her under his generous wing. 'She reminded me of my old mum,' he told me later. But Auntie May, alas, continued to be a difficult person to help. Realising that she was sleeping in a chair, Mr Jarvis cleared a space upstairs and began to build and furnish a bedroom for her, but she wouldn't sleep in it. He told me that when he showed it to her, all she said was that the carpet he had put down didn't belong in that room and that she couldn't sleep there anyway, as it was the guest room.

In March 1993, Tony and I took Auntie May's Dutch cousin, Mies, to visit her. Mies was about the same age as Auntie May, but by then, Auntie May was looking very much older. I hadn't seen Auntie May since the previous summer, when she had been bright and cheerful, but now, she looked sad, listless and weak. The grey hair that peeped out from under her headscarf was matted. Her skin was dry and looked dirty. She moved slowly and was clearly in pain. She invited us into the kitchen, so that we could sit in front of the Rayburn.

I have a sad and vivid memory of the scene. I remember her opening the fire-box, picking up a fragment of a rotten oak beam from the wood basket and setting it on the feebly glowing ashes in the grate. We sat there, surrounded by coats, jackets and dresses on hangers suspended from nails in the beams of the ceiling: the headless ghosts of Auntie May's past. The room was impossibly cluttered, even by Auntie May's standards. Every surface was covered in piles of empty jars and cans. I got out my daughter's wedding photographs. As I passed the photos to her, one by one, she peered at them. I noticed that her glasses were filthy. I wondered whether to offer to clean them for her, but feared she might take offence. She looked at a dozen or so pictures and made a comment on them; then, as she paused over one of them, we realised she had fallen asleep.

I remember thinking that she looked as if she was dying. Her face, her hair, her eyes, the pain she couldn't conceal, the clutter over which she had finally lost control – everything about her said: 'This is the end.' In the car on the way home, none of us felt like speaking. Mies broke the silence. 'Don't cry, Christine,' she said. 'May's not unhappy.' But all three of us knew that wasn't true.

CHAPTER EIGHTEEN

The Final Catastrophe

In which I describe the events surrounding
Auntie May's death

The catastrophe the doctor had foretold several years earlier came the very next day, and it was not minor. Auntie May was trying to light the paraffin stove in the great hall. It was cold, and she had arthritis in her fingers: she dropped a match. The floorboards under the stove must have been soaked by countless paraffin spills over the years and they caught fire immediately. She tried to beat out the flames with a towel, but they quickly spread. I know exactly what happened, because as luck would have it, Mr Jarvis was working upstairs at the time. He told me he heard May shriek and saw the flames through the gaps in the floorboards. He rushed down, ushered her into the garden and dialled 999.

When the firemen arrived, they couldn't get through the door with all their gear on. They smashed a window and threw out as much junk as they could in order to get in. When they reached the kitchen, they put out the flames quite quickly. Auntie May, meanwhile, was looking lost at the bottom of her garden, surrounded by brambles and nettles, clutching the collar of Muttley, who was barking furiously.

Meanwhile, an ambulance appeared. There was a nurse on

board, who spent a long time persuading Auntie May that she really needed to go to hospital, 'just for a check-up'. Shocked, frightened and exhausted, Auntie May finally gave in. Mr Jarvis assured her he would make sure the house and dog were looked after, and off she went.

The hospital told Nellie, who was her next of kin, but they passed on her instruction that nobody else was to be told, so Tony and I knew nothing of all this for nearly two weeks. We had a long-standing arrangement with Mr Jarvis that he would let us know if Auntie May ever needed us, but on the day of the accident, she had made him promise not to tell anyone what had happened. But when he visited her in the Wells Cottage Hospital, he could see how quickly she had declined, and he telephoned Tony and me to let us know. Poor Mr Jarvis! He clearly felt awful about breaking his word to Auntie May, who had trusted him so totally. But I am very glad he did.

I drove up to Wells immediately. Auntie May looked better than I had feared – better, indeed, than when I had seen her the day before the accident. At last, somebody was looking after her. She was propped up in a bed with fresh, white sheets, her ulcerated legs under a protective cage. Her eyes seemed small and sunken, but her skin was moist and waxy – almost translucent. Her hair had been washed and cut. She pushed it from her face with the back of her hand as she spoke.

The doctors hadn't told me what was wrong with her – she had forbidden them. When I asked her directly, she said that she was 'fine' and just needed a bit of a rest. It was obvious that this wasn't true, but I allowed myself to hope. I booked myself into the Normans Hotel and visited Auntie May daily until the end of the week. She had never been an easy person to chat to, but now, she seemed to drop her defences and began to tell me little stories from her past. I remember how when I mentioned the name of Polly's Polish husband, which was Kossowicz, she corrected my pronunciation. 'No! Not "Kossowicks", "Kossoff-itch". Like David Kossoff, the actor. He worked with me in De Havilland's, you know. We were good friends. He used to draw little cartoons in the margins of my technical drawings,' she said. When I told her that Tony and I had been on holiday in Wales and had visited the fairytale seaside village built by a famous architect, I couldn't remember the name of the place – but Auntie May came straight out with it: 'Portmeirion,' she said. 'Built by Clough Williams Ellis.' However ill she might have been, her mind was still sharp.

The doctors said her condition was stable, so I felt it was OK to go home. It was just about the only time I ever did leave her knowing that she was comfortable and safe, but a couple of days later, the hospital telephoned to say that they thought I ought to come back, and come back quickly. They didn't say so, but when I got there, it was obvious: Auntie May was dying, and dying fast.

•

Auntie May's will told us precisely what to do with all her possessions, but said nothing at all about what she wanted done with her body. It seemed odd at the time, but I now see it as one of many signs of her selflessness. She was cremated locally and her ashes laid in her mother's grave in Pinner cemetery. Later, when I found that she had marked every anniversary of her mother's death in her diaries, I knew that we had done the right thing. Auntie May was at peace.

CHAPTER NINETEEN

Restored to Life

In which I describe what happened to the house – and
to me – after Auntie May's death

Tony and I spent the next six years working together on the house.
It wasn't easy. To begin with, we would leave our own cottage in
Cambridgeshire every Friday evening, spend the weekend in Wells
and return on Sunday night. Progress was slow. After we realised
that the project needed more time and more money spent on it, and
I gave up my teaching job and moved permanently into Ware Hall-
House, I became general gofer and dogsbody, preparer and
finisher. I plastered (not very flat, not very smooth, but with
mediaeval-looking results!). I cleared the tangled forest of the
garden. I ordered the building materials and made sure they were
ready for Tony when he turned up at the weekend to carry out the
heavier work. 'We didn't get the house,' he used to say. 'The house
got us.'

But it got us in different ways. I felt that I had to do more than
just finish the building – I had to carry on and complete Auntie
May's life. That was the meaning of the promise that I had made to
her on her deathbed, though I hadn't realised it at the time. For
me, it was a responsibility that became a joy. For Tony, though, it
was a burden that became increasingly irksome. Looking back, I

can see why. He still had a full-time job. We had spent most of our married life rebuilding and renovating our own house and, at a time when we should have been thinking about retirement, he had been saddled with another one to restore – one that he didn't own, one that he hadn't chosen and one that he had many times said he didn't want.

Then there was the expense. In 1997, Tony said we needed to sit down and think about things. It no longer made sense for us to run two houses at once. Apart from anything else, we couldn't afford to. He suggested selling The Nook and buying a bachelor flat, but I saw it as a chance to do something more romantic – to buy a boat that we could both enjoy together. Tony agreed, and we bought a handsome vintage Dutch barge in Holland, sailed it around the Ijsselmeer and then eventually moored it at the Fish and Duck, near Ely. Tony lived on it during the week and joined me most weekends.

Then, out of the blue, he was made redundant. I thought this was wonderful – now, we could be together full time in Wells and moor our boat in the harbour. But it didn't work out like that. Shortly after he rejoined me full time in Ware Hall-House, I found out that he had been leading another life – a simpler, easier life that didn't involve the complexities that had been thrust upon him. He had another woman. When I found out, my world fell apart. I had been faithful to him for nearly 40 years. He had been my only love – my only real boyfriend since the age of fifteen. I had a nervous breakdown.

The Savidge sisters saved my sanity. I went to live with dear Nellie, who was then a widow in her mid-nineties. Tony had left us both and we looked after each other, finding solace in our mutual loss. I was never really quite sure who was helping whom, but we muddled through our traumas together and shared many thoughts and memories of May. They were very different characters. May could never part with anything; Nellie pared her possessions down to an absolute minimum. There was nothing in the house that wasn't used. There were two knives, two forks, and two spoons in the kitchen drawer. There were two cups, two saucers and two plates in the sideboard. There were two sets of sheets for each bed – one for use and one for the wash. Every tabletop and cupboard surface was clear of clutter. Nellie and May were poles apart in character, but I came to realise that they were poles of the same planet. They were both obsessive about *things* – May couldn't part with them and Nellie wouldn't be burdened with them. Now, I wonder whether this reflects their damaged childhood – the poverty that followed the death of their father, the succession of lodging houses that were never their own home, the loss of the family furniture and possessions . . . does this explain their obsessiveness? I can only guess. I was with Nellie for just a year before she developed cancer and died. I was heartbroken. She was like a second mother to me.

I returned to Wells and began my task again in earnest, converting my anger at what had happened to me into energy that I used in hard work. Friends and family rallied round. They helped me to landscape the garden: it now has a parterre, with four tonnes of slate chippings surrounding a little fountain. I helped to fit new bathrooms. They helped to build an extension – an orangery. It wasn't part of May's original plan, but I would like to think she would be pleased by it – it's a little bit of me that I wanted to contribute to the house. When the time comes for the house to pass to my children, Daniel and Polly, no doubt they will add something of themselves, too. But the building will always be Auntie May's memorial and there are permanent reminders of her everywhere. The beams still have her marks upon them; her mends, where she cut out rotten wood and pegged in pieces she had cut with her own hands, still whisper her name.

The place is peaceful. Once, when people called at the front door, they were greeted by the snarling and growling of May's dog; now, they enter to the sound of an old-fashioned bell on a spring. They step into a corridor that is no longer crammed with jam jars, furniture and boxes, but is an airy passage some 30ft in height. Above it, they see a galleried landing with a ladder-stair to the attic floor, where I now store most of May's boxes and trunks.

Downstairs, two mahogany doors open onto the great hall, with heavy beams and an inglenook fireplace. Half the room is filled with a grand boardroom table. I am sitting at it now. Under it, my feet are touching more of May's boxes — the ones that contain the diaries and papers I have used in writing this book. On the far side of the room, a door leads to what used to be the bakery. The space is now a hall, utility room and bathroom, but the shop window is still there. It used to stand on the narrow pavement of the main road in Ware, with traffic rushing by, but now it overlooks an ancient apple tree in a sleepy garden, where the only sounds are birdsong and the buzzing of bees. The house has retired, and is quiet and contented at last.

A few years ago, an elderly lady and her son knocked on the front door and introduced themselves. She told me she had lived above the bakery when newly married. I invited them in for tea, and when we stood in what had been her old bedroom, she told me that the window had overlooked the cobbled courtyard of the pub next door. Now, you see a moss-covered folly that we built to look like the ruins of a mediaeval monastery. The son asked if Auntie May had found any marbles when she had dismantled the house. She had: a whole jarful. He and his brother had played marbles in their bedroom, he said, and had lost many between the floorboards and the ceiling below. 'Was there a red one?' he said. There was.

Past the inside balcony is my own bedroom, which was originally the 'solar', the sleeping area of the mediaeval house. It has a large, arched, leaded window that we found in the garden. Another bedroom is behind a secret door in a false bookcase. People say it contributes to the fairytale feel of the house. I suppose it does. The windows do, too. They are all of different shapes, sizes and ages. Sometimes, it seems as if the house hasn't been frozen in time, but has frozen time itself. There are mirrors everywhere – I wanted to bring in more light – and in many places it is difficult to tell what is real from what is reflected. A bed-and-breakfast guest making a return visit said she had half expected to follow the wall down the lane to find that there was no longer a gate in it and that her first stay had happened in a dream.

The house certainly has its own personality. It even has its own voice, but it is a voice that has mellowed. When the wind blew, the frame would rock and the oak joints would let out creaking, graunching squeaks; I haven't heard them since we stabilised it by building internal buttresses. One or two windows still leak, including the skylight that Auntie May made from old fish boxes. But I live with it. Auntie May's copper jugs and preserving pans catch the plinking, plonking drips. On wet days, soft music made by rainwater plays gently through the house.

Most visitors catch their breath as they come through the front door. When the BBC's *Antiques Roadshow* came to Norfolk in May 2006, I invited them to come and see a piece of her furniture, a desk with a connection to the American author Mark Twain. They sent antiques expert Paul Atterbury to look at it, but when I opened the door to him, he said: 'Never mind the desk, what about the house?' He was bowled over by what he saw and persuaded me to appear on the show to tell Auntie May's story. Later, he chose Ware Hall-House as his 'favourite find' in a *Roadshow* special broadcast in 2007.

On each occasion, letters from viewers flooded in. Some came from people who had known Auntie May when she lived in Ware, or had met her after her move to Wells – they were all proud to have met or known her and wanted to share their memories. Since then, as the programmes are shown in country after country, a stream of letters from overseas have been arriving. So many came that I wondered whether I should be replying to them all. I rang the programme's secretary for advice. 'What do people do when this happens?' I asked. 'Well,' she said, 'it doesn't, usually.'

But then Auntie May was an unusual character. Tony had been wrong when he had accused me of turning into her. I couldn't have endured what she had put up with – living through all those winters in the leaky shell of a house in which the temperature fell below freezing for weeks at a time; never getting a full night's sleep in a bed, but dozing fitfully in a chair; living on a diet of bread, bananas, packet soup and biscuits; suffering constant pain from ulcers that never healed, without complaining – no, I could never do that. I can't think of anyone who could. The only other people that I can think of who might have put up with such things were the ancient saints. The difference, I suppose, is that those saints went out of their way to find suffering; Auntie May just encountered it and coped. I think that makes her pretty saintly, too.

Now that I am at the end of telling her story, I find myself thinking of so many things that I haven't mentioned. Many of them would warrant a chapter in their own right. I haven't described the tin box containing snippets of the black and white films in which Denis Elliot Watson had acted. I haven't told the story of the 'Cupie' doll: Nellie had owned it when a child and had thrown it away after it had been broken. May rescued it and kept it, and Nellie next saw it ninety years later. I haven't said anything about the antique paraffin projector with a whole set of Victorian missionaries' slides illustrating the perils of the demon drink – where did that come from? I haven't described the four ancient typewriters, the collection of nineteenth-century Valentine's cards, the chocolate boxes filled with sets of cigarette cards, the silk-tied Chinese books of woodcuts of birds, animal and insects, or the suitcases filled with fragments of antique Dutch lace. I haven't written of Auntie May's friendship – was it more? – with Captain Ricketts, the sailor, who died of flu in 1953. I haven't mentioned finding and trying on a trunkful of beautiful nineteenth-century dresses and discovering that they fitted me perfectly. I haven't described my pleasure at finding the very dress worn by Auntie May's friend Emily, in the portrait that hangs in the cross-passage, or my delight when, years later, I came across the necklace that she wore in it, too. And there's something else I haven't said that I should have: I haven't said how much I owe to Auntie May. I'll say it now.

Auntie May: your building project gave me a real sense of purpose when I desperately needed one. Retracing the steps of your life rekindled mine. Reading your diaries and going through your possessions, there were times when what I found made me weep; but there were also times when I could almost feel you pulling at my sleeve, inviting me to look here, or there, and see the many fascinating things that you valued and stored away so long ago. It seems a lifetime ago that I was standing by your bedside, pledging to do whatever you had left to be done. Your house is calm now: it's warm, and it's comfortable. Your task is complete – and now, so is mine. Your last word to me was 'Sorry'. It shouldn't have been. I want my last words to you to be 'Thank you'.

Index